IT'S THE
WILL,
NOT THE
SKILL

IT'S THE
WILL,
NOT THE
SKILL

PRINCIPLES AND PHILOSOPHIES OF SUCCESS

As Seen Through the Eyes, Mind and Heart of

HERM EDWARDS
Head Coach of the Kansas City Chiefs

Revised Edition

A book for leaders: parents, teachers, coaches
and managers who strive to build self-confidence
and improve the performance of others.

Jim Tunney, Ed.D.

IT'S THE WILL, NOT THE SKILL
Revised Edition

Published by
Executive Books
206 West Allen Street
Mechanicsburg, PA 17055
717-766-9499 800-233-2665
Fax: 717-766-6565
www.ExecutiveBooks.com

Copyright © 2007 by Jim Tunney

ISBN-13: 978-1-933715-48-3

ISBN-10: 1-933715-48-0

Book Production Services Provided by Gregory Dixon

Cover Photo by Hank Young, Kansas City Chiefs' Photographer

Printed in the United States of America

CONTENTS

DEDICATION

This book is dedicated to the parents of Coach Herman Edwards. His father, Herman Sr., a career army master sergeant who died in 1978 always told him, "Son, I can't give you lots of money or a fancy home, but I can give you a good name. Use it wisely." Martha, his mother, lives in their California home today and promotes the Edwards code.

ACKNOWLEDGEMENTS

E very writing effort is a T*E*A*M approach, and every author is grateful for his/her supporters. The writing of this book was definitely a collaborative effort. When the project began in January 2002, John Oldach, a Hollywood screenwriter, provided wonderful ideas and syntax in crafting chapter titles and context. Janet Peck was a valuable resource as she transcribed the taping of the interviews.

Herman's mother, Martha; his wife, Lia; his son, Marcus; and his sister, Irvina were most supportive and helpful in providing pictures and family history. In writing about Herman's life in Monterey, California, I had the help of Jim Cota, Dan Albert, Mike Chapman, Joe Bommarito, Luke Phillips, Chris Pappas, and a score of others who, as coaches and friends, provided insights to his athletic ability that matured into his support of his community.

In writing about the professional world of Herman, as an athlete as well as a coach, I owe a debt of gratitude for the cooperation of the Jets and Chiefs media staff and personnel who provided content, pictures and assistance in helping describe the essence of Coach Edwards. Every one—from the security guard to their owners—has only positive things to say about Herman as a person, a leader and a friend.

Some of these are Terry Bradway, former NY Jets' General Manager; Paul Hackett, former Jets' Offensive Coordinator; Carl Peterson, Kansas City Chiefs' President; Mike White, Herman's college coach; Marty Schottenheimer, former Head Coach of Kansas City Chiefs and San Diego Chargers; Tony Dungy, Head Coach Indianapolis Colts; Ron Jaworski, Philadelphia Eagles quarterback and Herman's teammate.

Support in putting this manuscript together was provided by Anna

Mitchell, who typed (entered into our computer database) endlessly to perfect each sentence, each paragraph. And finally, the wonderful support and encouragement from my wife, Linda, who put up with long hours of desk work and travel to secure the best story possible.

You Have to Have the Will

Vince Lombardi is quoted as saying: "Winning is not a sometime thing; it's an all-the-time thing. You don't win once in a while, you don't do things right once in a while, you do them right all the time. Winning is a habit. Unfortunately, so is losing.

"There is no room for second place. There is only one place in my game and that is first place. I have finished second twice in my time at Green bay and I don't ever want to finish second again. There is a second place bowl game, but it is a game for losers played by losers. It is and always has been an American zeal to be first in anything we do and to win and to win and to win.

"Every time a football player goes out to ply his trade he's got to play from the ground up—from the soles of his feet right up to his head. Every inch of him has to play. Some guys play with their heads— that's O.K. You've got to be smart to be No. 1 in any business. But more important, you've got to play with your heart—with every fiber of your body. If you're lucky enough to find a guy with a lot of head and a lot of heart, he's never going to come off the field second.

"Running a football team is no different from running any other kind of organization—an army, a political party, a business. The principles are the same. The object is to win—to beat the other guy. Maybe that sounds hard or cruel. I don't think it is.

"It's a reality of life that men are competitive and the most competitive games draw the most competitive men. That's why they're there—to compete. They know the rules and the objectives when they get in the game. The objective is to win—fairly, squarely, decently, by the rules—but to win.

"And in truth, I've never known a man worth his salt who in the long run, deep down in his heart, didn't appreciate the grind, the discipline.

There is something in good men that really yearns for, needs, discipline and the harsh reality of head-to-head combat.

"I don't say these things because I believe in the 'brute' nature of man or that men must be brutalized to be combative. I believe in God, and I believe in human decency. But I firmly believe that any man's finest hour—his greatest fulfillment to all he holds dear—is that moment when he has worked his heart out in a good cause and lies exhausted on the field of battle—victorious."

Vincent Thomas Lombardi was born in Brooklyn on June 11, 1913, the son of an immigrant Italian butcher. He is best known as the legendary coach of the Green Bay Packers. In his playing days at Fordham University, he was one of the seven Blocks of Granite. Although he was a successful coach in high school and college as well as an assistant coach in the NFL, fame did not reach Lombardi until he took the head coaching job of the Green Bay Packers.

The Packers were floundering when Lombardi was hired to be their head coach (in 1959). Under his leadership the Packers won five world championships in his nine seasons at Green Bay. The first two Super Bowls (then called the World Championship Game) were a landmark victory for Lombardi's Packers. In Super Bowl I, the Packers defeated the AFL Champions Kansas City Chiefs 35-10; followed the next year with the Packers beating the Oakland Raiders 33-14. These two victories lifted Lombardi and the Packers to a special place in the history of professional football.

"Coach"—as his players were wont to call him—died of cancer September 3, 1970. Although many decades have passed, Lombardi is still revered as the man who said: "The will to excel and the will to win, they endure."

INTRODUCTION

Herman Edwards Jr. spent most of his youth and early adult life living on the Monterey, California Peninsula. He attended Highland Elementary, Martin Luther King Junior High School, Monterey High School and Monterey Peninsula College—all in that area.

His father, Herman Edwards Sr., now deceased, was a master sergeant stationed at Fort Ord, California, located on the Monterey Peninsula. His mother, Martha, still lives on the peninsula. The genesis of Herman's values, beliefs and daily practices stem from these two.

Many of Herman Jr.'s life-learning experiences are the focus of this book. This is not so much of a biography, and yet each person who touched Herman's life has contributed to his history. Of primary interest is in the vignette about "The Broom."

Herm tells it this way:

When I was six or seven my job at our house was to sweep up the leaves. Late one November when the leaves had pretty much covered our backyard, I eagerly went about my job to sweep up the leaves. (Remember I said "sweep up" not "rake" since our thirty-by-thirty-feet backyard was cement not grass.)

Anyway, I thought I had done a good job and was proud of that day's task, so I left the leaves all piled up in the center of our yard and rushed into the house to tell my dad. I said, "Dad, Dad, I've got all the leaves swept up in a pile. I want you to see!" My chest was puffed up with pride. My dad, master sergeant that he was and with no extra effort to mount any further military assertiveness, walked down the steps of our back porch and "paraded" about the yard.

"Herman," he said. "Look, you left some leaves here in this corner."

I stammered, "But—but—Dad—"

13

He kept on talking, "And this corner a few more leaves."

I finally got a chance to speak and said, "But, Dad, there are just a couple—several was more like it—of leaves in those corners." And then in my young but convincing voice said, "Nobody will notice those leaves way over in that corner."

Dad never hesitated, and with stern but encouraging words said, "Herman, you gotta get the corners!" He continued with that strong and military commanding voice, "Son, he paused, don't be afraid of the broom!"

Herman got the message without another word from Dad. The message was that in doing your job, do every detail (the corners) successfully. He learned that "the broom" is just a metaphor for diligence and correctness in achieving peak performance.

Every task he undertook thereafter, from household chores to organizing a pick-up team on the playground to his days as an athlete—everything he did and does to this day—he always thinks of "the broom" to show the way to doing his best.

Incidentally, while Herm always wanted to be an end (now called receiver, wide receiver or wide out) in football, he played "cornerback" throughout high school, college, and into the pros! His father's words, "You gotta get the corners," was more than just a metaphor; it became his "ticket" to being a professional athlete and head coach.

The Official's Call

I first became aware of No. 46 Herm Edwards of the Philadelphia Eagles when I moved to the Monterey Peninsula in 1980. As you will read in chapter 8, Herm and Mike Chapman asked me to MC their golf tournaments that would raise money to build a new boys club on the Monterey Peninsula. I didn't even play golf in those days but his "cause" was such a worthy one that I eagerly joined their "mission" with that event and those that followed. Herman and I became close friends and today we both serve on each other's foundation boards. The purpose of this book is to honor Herman, his family and his community extolling the principles and philosophies that not only he teaches, but lives by. I believe the positive message of this book will help others. Although much of this book is about Herm's first head coaching job with the Jets (2001-2005), he brought the same principles to the Chiefs when he became head coach in 2006.

CHAPTER 1

Speed Bumps

Rejection is just missing success by about a hair or two.

—Herm Edwards

Analyzing the New York Jets during the first two years of his tenure as a head coach, a wide variety of impressions can be formed. The New York press has not shied from the task of identifying any of these, and they've been joined by a national corps of TV and print journalists as the Jets have matured and solidified as a team. But in all the coverage the Jets have received, the predominant impression formed is the simplest one based on fact: this was a team that refused to roll over. Rebounding from a 2-5 start in 2002, key injuries, quarterback transitions, and plain bad luck, the team had proven to be tough enough to keep showing up, and skillful enough to exploit the opportunities thus presented. "The only time you quit is when you retire," is what Coach Edwards told John Devine of the Monterey Herald, and for him that line is like describing the difference between forward and reverse to someone who has never operated a motor vehicle. It's a simple maxim that can spell the difference between arriving somewhere and becoming a ditch-bound statistic.

Late in the 2002 season, after the Jets beat the Green Bay Packers convincingly in the final regular-season game, Coach Edwards met with the cordon of writers and broadcasters that always congregate in the tidied-up corner of the clubhouse that serves as the briefing area. It had been a long climb to get there, on good footing going into the postseason, and they were mindful of every step taken. Nothing was taken for granted, but they had also refused to accept a lesser definition of their team when on-the-field evidence might have suggested it.

And one way or another, they reconstructed the season and found themselves feeling good after that Green Bay game. There was no sudden burst upon the scene like ringers from another solar system, as some in the room might have described it in order to beef up interest or controversy and sell more sports sections.

Herm reflected this in his initial remarks, telling the stadium press corps, "Someone said the season was over. But I wasn't smart enough to know that and the players weren't dumb enough to listen. It just shows what perseverance gets for you when you believe in each other and just go out and try to win the game." It was the umpteenth repetition of the old message, but it sounded fresh coming from a club that had just defeated some daunting odds.

Herm faced that challenge more than once in his ambition to be an NFL player and a coach. A major disappointment confronted him after his freshman year at University of California, and he decided it best to leave that team.

As you will read in succeeding chapters, he wouldn't let his ambition to play college football fade away. So a restart at Monterey Peninsula College, then a solid season at San Diego State reaffirmed that ambition. Then disappointment happened again when he was not drafted by any NFL team. However, another door opened when he "walked on" as a free agent with the Philadelphia Eagles.

After a ten-year NFL-playing career, Herm wanted to coach. Claude Gilbert, his San Diego State coach, had moved to San Jose State and asked Herm to join his staff as a Defensive Backs Coach. After two years at that job, Herm felt the situation was not right. Disappointed and somewhat discouraged he returned home to "think it over." At home in order to give himself a chance at repositioning, he built model tanks—a childhood activity that he always loved (Herman Edwards Sr. was a mechanic who worked on army tanks.) Meanwhile he talked to many friends in town and considered going to work at a van and storage company and maybe help coach at Monterey Peninsula College—his alma mater. It was this time when—bam!—another opportunity presented itself with the call from Carl Peterson of the Kansas City Chiefs, which launched itself into an opportunity to work toward his coaching ambition. More on that later.

Adversity is a given. You want a first down, fine—you only need to persuade the eleven snarling men on the other side of that line to move ten yards in a different direction. You want to find a new job with great benefits, excellent—steel your ears for numerous repetitions of the word "no." You want to experience the elation of finishing a marathon, wonderful—but the only route to it is through miles eighteen to twenty-three. You want to house train your puppy, terrific—don't cancel the paper. There's being no way around this condition in life. How do we adjust to it? There have been hundreds of millions of words devoted to this question, across the pages of a never-ending stream of books, over the tops of countless podiums, spoken by a nearly infinite variety of encouragers. Yet all of these messages have a single, rugged command in common. It is the heart of all progress, and it can be expressed with the utmost simplicity in three short words: *Don't give up.*

Gut Check

The descending sun appears to be struggling for survival, hanging itself in the treetops beyond left-center field and sending out a final burst of blinding rays. The eleven-year old batter backs out of the box and screws his helmet down tighter on his head, squinting out of his left eye at the third-base coach, then at the gangly pitcher sweating on the mound. He steps back into the box with the expression of a man trying to put a rattlesnake in a gunnysack. Dirt-streaked hands find their grip on the bat as the umpire pushes up his chest protector and sinks to his observation posture.

The young pitcher blows out more air than he took in his last inhale, flicking a nervous eye toward the runner at third. The beautiful game that seemed to glow in the April dusk just two innings ago has evolved into something else entirely. The two-hitter he had going has stretched into seven plus, with enough booted balls in the infield and subsequent wild pitches to erase a three-run lead and replace it with a four-run deficit.

He rears back in a full windup, ignoring the runner taking off for a second lest the petty larceny spoil the direction and velocity of the fastball he intends to deliver.

But still the theft bothers him, burns a little, and makes him hesitate ever so slightly before he releases the ball. As it approaches the batter his knuckles turn white in restraint of lashing too soon at this plump offering, which rolls through the air like a horsehide bowling ball. The batter holds off until the pitch has become a still life on the west edge of the plate. Then he swings with a grunt, and the ball is redirected into left field, a long way from any welcoming leather. One run scores, then another as the base thief scampers home. The short-stop relays the ball to second base where it is both late and dropped, and the batter steams into third feeling legendary.

The pitcher trudges back to the mound from behind home plate, with footsteps that describe an exhausting and hopeless journey. He slaps at the ball with his glove as it returns to him. Every movement he makes seems to declare that the world stinks and only suckers care, but his mother can detect the faint tremor in his lower lip from where she sits five aluminum steps up on the first-base side. When he was much smaller, she'd gather him in and rock him gently in moments like these. But now she can only make her hands busy by fiddling with her sunglasses, and call out her son's name in a plea for courage.

The boy's coach, leaning against the dugout fence, also sees the dejection temporarily infecting his ace. Uncrossing his arms, he sig-nals for time and takes a deliberate stroll to the mound. Making the dirt dome as private as possible, he places a hand on the kid's throw-ing shoulder and tries to help him turn the trembling lip into the bot-tom half of some kind of smile.

"I had Schilling and Johnson warming up for you, but they went to the ice cream truck and I haven't seen 'em since," he jokes, lamely. The pitcher retreats from his funk just long enough to register his mock disgust with the coach's not-ready-for-primetime humor. The coach sees his opening and slips in. "Hey, we're running out of day-light and I can tell that the ump wants to go straight home and sit in his easy chair. We have to get one more at-bat. Let's figure this out, okay? All right then, let's bear down and get these last two outs," says the coach with a soothing growl. "And let's have fun doing it! You guys back him up. We're still in this thing."

When Herm searches his personal history for the source of his determination to stay the course and keep fighting, to scrap and maneuver and survive, he invariably invokes the memory of his father, Herman Edwards Sr.'s, philosophy, which demanded disci-plined concentration in the face of all obstacles. His dad would say, "Son, there's a point where you can get excited, but when you lose focus on what you're doing it's no good. Because then you can be had. You always have to keep your thoughts and your present faculties on the picture in front of you." Undoubtedly, he learned that from being a soldier.

This message has echoed and re-echoed through Herm's consciousness to the point where response to misadventure is reflective. He learned to trust himself in situations where trouble is either brewing or boiling. This can encourage an inner calmness which, given a chance, can find its way out and have an effect on external events. Coach Edwards always tells the players, "Don't panic. Whatever you do, don't panic." He really doesn't like to be around people who panic. Of course, the same goes for him. When you're the head guy, you have to set the tone. You always want to keep your composure. In the heat of a battle, when life's challenges are stated in the extreme, to lose composure is to invite—to nearly guarantee—problems greater than the ones you already had. He knew that as a player, when he played the corner. Things can get out of hand very quickly. If you can think clearly, generally you're going to be the person who comes out of the situation in reasonable shape. You don't want to be making hasty decisions when desperation is controlling all the information you use. And it's one of those deals—"you never want them to see you sweat." His father may not have been the first man to speak those words but he might as well have been. For Herm, he certainly made them his own, and like any good son he credits his father with authorship.

From his father he learned reason in the face of setback and how it applies to life. For a more specific application of this attitude, in the professional world he came to know best, he examined Tom Landry, the late great coach of the Dallas Cowboys. Standing tall and reserved on the sideline, topped by his famous trademark hat, he brought the same even demeanor to every situation he encountered as a coach. In rain, snow, or shine, ahead or behind, Landry surveyed the field as the calmest person in the stadium. Game officials would appear feverish in comparison to the dignified coach with the deep Texan drawl. A generation of Americans (especially males of the football-loving variety) came of age when Landry instilled in their minds the picture of unflappability. Herm watched Landry on the sidelines and was in awe of him. Here's a guy who never loses his temper. How can he do that? How is that humanly possible?

He'd never lose his temper, and yet he had control of his team.

And it was always a good, competitive team playing under him. Herm watched him, analyzed, and looked for angles and cracks in that armor. You see, Herm had a temper growing up. He didn't like to lose, and he was kind of opinionated; the images of Landry and him were not exactly one and the same. But as he got older he began to question himself more, and he saw the wisdom of coaching like Landry, one of not losing composure. The more Herm ventured into the field of professional coaching, the more he wanted to make that one of his strengths.

It's a short run of dominoes: losing composure leads to losing focus, and this is the worst fate that can befall a winning effort. But as prescription for that, Coach Edwards believes and teaches that winning and losing are sometimes separated by the thinnest of margins. You have to learn how to handle losing before you can win. Because then you understand that winning and losing are closely related. You need to be able to sit with yourself in the aftermath of a defeat and deal with the practical truth of your effort. You have to have the integrity to accept the answers to the question, "Well, why did I lose?" And losing composure is frequently a sign that a competitor has abdicated personal responsibility for his or her effort. It's a form of shaking our fists at heaven and furiously demanding our "due." It's a surefire way to add to the distance between you and whatever it will take to win. When you start pointing fingers, no matter how fast you are on the draw, there will always be three of them pointing back at you. That's when you let the team carry you. It's never one person's loss alone. Whatever your situation is, you can always find a team there. Even when you're standing alone, the resources for backup are already in you.

No matter what level of competition you're involved in— whether it's professional football or Pop Warner, whether you're good or mediocre, a girl or a boy, wearing new shoes or beat-up ones—the word "win" has to mean something. It has to be worth some sacrifice. That word can't be bought with discount coupons. You have to earn it. That's something we need to remember when we fall short. Maybe the time wasn't right. Or maybe we didn't take enough time to prepare. Whatever the reason, it helps to recall the first law of consumerism: you get what you pay for. And when it comes to winning, we don't want the cheap stuff we want the real deal. We want the stuff we bought with sweat and smarts, with character and readiness. When we lose, we may have brought all that out only to discover that we couldn't exchange it for victory. That's the "hair or two" that separates success and rejection. It's imperative that we maintain enough common sense and dignity to make a clear evaluation of why we didn't get all the way to our desired result. That job belongs to us. And whatever our investigation reveals, we have to know that if we left our best effort on the field, then something good will follow. Going out and putting everything we've got into an effort is always a correct first step on the way to something better.

It's important to spend as much time analyzing defeats as victories. There's no denying that the toughest day of the week is when you've lost a game and you come back in on Monday. It's tough, but it's necessary, because there needs to be a reckoning. We can all imagine situations, many of them, from daily life with our jobs, our families, and our outside activities, where perhaps events and decisions skittered away from our firm control. At those times, a little objectivity can go a long way. In football context, it follows a particular sequence that actually becomes a rebuilding ritual. You get the game film, and you watch it. You watch and you identify the little things that got you beat. Then you get yourself in the right frame of mind, and you make sure that your staff is on that page with you, and then you all turn around and try to get the players where they need to be. Because somebody in all this madness has to be positive and have a firm hand. Coach Edwards is not about to let the team think that everything's fine after a loss, any more than they should assume that they're entitled to win just because they got dressed and went out on the field.

In the dynamic of a football game, allowances are made for the self-analysis described here. "Halftime is a failure management course built right into the game," says Edwards. Whatever has preceded the break at thirty minutes, a team is given the opportunity to retreat to a haven free from the battle and reassemble its resources. If a team has been successful, they are given a chance to build on that advantage. If they have struggled or have been caught unprepared in some aspect of its game plan, the crash course is about what they were doing wrong, along with a chance to start over. This chance to start over is often all that an eventual winner needs.

Gut Check

The kid rolls the ball lightly in his right hand and looks at his catcher's target like it is an English reading assignment that he's shirked all week. Now would be a good time to get caught just closed, no more tours. With the third out recorded, the fielders all dash for the dugout, patting their ace on the back as they run by enjoying their victory. There's not much daylight left.

Toward the end of a challenging season in the NFL, with only so many playoff spots to go around, the action certainly intensifies. That's what the NFL is all about. It's about good players rising up and telling everyone else, "Climb on my back, because we're moving ahead and I'll take you there." Whether we like it or not, the losses become more significant. After each week there are a couple of new tenants down in the basement, looking up and hoping that fate will twist a certain way for them, that luck will come in and fill in the hope where their effort was supposed to go like a penny in a fuse box. And the people who keep winning are able to control their destiny. We already know that the difference between the two is not necessarily a big one. But there will be some consistent contrasts.

The people who keep going are the ones who roll up their sleeves and welcome the challenge. These are the people who embrace the chaos and work together. These are the teams that have found a large element of their identity in facing adversity together. You never know in the game of football, and that's one of the great things about it. The front office does its job; hires the people it believes are needed, and gets them all together. "Everybody comes to training camp and starts from ground zero. You have high expectations, obviously, because if you don't, you're done before you cover your first kickoff. This is a belief business," Coach Edwards often reminds his players.

But getting the good players on the field together with a good bunch of coaches isn't enough. And talking it up, taking the lip tour to the Super Bowl is not going to work either. Edwards says, "You have to go play, pure and simple. And you play to win!" When you do that, especially at the level of the NFL, you are going to meet adversity. Adversity will show up like the building inspector when you've got more than two pickups and a stack of lumber parked in front of your house. Coach Edwards prefers to get to it early with his team, because it is the most important ingredient in the chemistry of a tight, successful team.

The playoff-bound Jets in the 2002 season found that out. They worked through training camp and started the season with the greatest of intentions, but those intentions were based on abstract things like reputations and impressions and "the buzz" on what certain guys might do for the team. It wasn't until they had fallen into a hole and couldn't seem to climb out of in the first half of the season that the team forged its identity.

The Jets didn't know who they were until they faced something that shook the foundation. And that brought them together in a way that nothing else had; it got them to the place where they could win. Winning changed everything. It brought the freedom and the confidence to just go out and win some more. Their thinking was, "If it's such a thin line between winning and losing, we might as well win."

Coach Edwards had been telling them that they had the talent to turn things around, but that was not news to anybody on that team. You don't play professional football because of how sharp you look in a uniform. You arrive at this level because you have demonstrated the talent to play better than the overwhelming majority of other guys who also played in college. The natural ability to perform at a high level is a given, but desire and determination don't always fall into that same category. So during one team meeting, Herm took them down memory lane as a football team, and pulled out the players' handbook and pointed out where it said *"It's the will, not the skill."* They had been focusing on the skill and just figuring to do the things they wanted to do. They were so fired up with all the new guys coming in and were starting out where they had left off after a 9-7 season in 2001. But they had to find the will to win, and that didn't really happen until they found themselves at 1-3, having been outscored 104-13 in three straight losses. That's when the light came on. That's when the Jets let go of all the hype and began to concentrate on the will. They looked around and found it in each other, and a winning football team began to emerge.

Edwards may have considered himself overly excitable in his early days, but by the time he was playing high school football his grace under fire was noticeable to his coaches. Ex-assistant Sal Cardinale chuckles in admiration of the soothing energy brought to the Monterey High squad by its star defensive back. "I can't think of any occasion where we ever had to sit him down or discipline him in the years we had him," he recalls. "Nothing. But I'll tell you what he did for me. It's Herman's senior year, and we're in the midst of a great season, with a big game coming up, and so Dan (Albert, the head coach) did a great thing to spark them for it. He went out and bought them all new jerseys, and the night of the game he goes to the gym and passes them out. The kids are pumped up, and everything was phenomenal, just flying high.

"One guy, though, was really angry because he didn't get the number he wanted," Cardinale continues. "He started in complaining, and he wouldn't stop. We're doing some things on the chalkboard in the gym as we're trying to prepare ourselves for a real test of the team, and there's all this moaning and negative stuff coming from this kid. I got really angry for one of the very few times in my coaching experience. I looked back and threw the chalk against the wall and stomped right out of the gym. I was so burned up that this guy was concerned about a number on a jersey rather than the game, and even worse, that his attitude was infecting me, and, by extension, the whole team.

"I'm outside by the big oak tree on our campus trying to cool off, and then the door opens up and here comes old Herman. Big smile on his face. 'Coach, coach, you can't do that. Relax.' That guy really irritated me, I told Herman. 'You know how he is,' Herman responded. 'Cries a little bit to get his way, and then he pipes down. We'll take care of it. Relax. You've got to enjoy the game tonight.' Here's an eighteen-year-old kid comforting me. He's turning me around. He was the person all the kids looked up to. He had that carriage, you know, and that smile that disarms anybody and everybody who's around him."

Tony Dungy is no stranger to this way of thinking, and he shares Edwards's fidelity to behavior that can set the stage for good things to happen—or at least, for there to be no regret about the outcome. "Herman's whole outlook is just positive," Dungy declares. "It fills the atmosphere around him with the idea that 'we are going to make it happen, and we won't worry about the obstacles. We'll just worry about how to overcome them.' He's something special that way." The two men shared a number of ups and downs together as fellow coaches in Kansas City and Tampa Bay; their relationship weighted more with the substance of mentor-friend than boss-underling. When it was time for Edwards to strike out on his own as a head coach, Dungy's final piece of advice to him concerned dealing with what Dungy considers to be one of coaching's biggest challenges.

"After training camp you've got more people than you need," Dungy observes. "You've got to cut some people. That's the toughest thing for a coach, and I told him it would be the toughest thing with the Jets. I'm sure it was, and is. As we would talk about that, the thing we always stressed was that number one, you know you have to do what's best for the team. When you have that requirement in place, it helps you in making your decisions. But I saw in Tampa Bay how positive he was with the guys that we would have to let go, and I know that's how he's going about it now. It's a tough thing for a pro player to hear, but there's a lesson on both sides of the decision to cut somebody.

"You want to tell the guy 'Hey, don't look at this as the end of the line, even if you decide to get out of football. It's still a beginning for you. What are you going to do with your life? Take what you learned here, and either put it toward your next chance to play, or put it toward what you eventually want to do with your life. The possibilities always lie ahead of you, not behind you.'"

Joe Bommarito has Edwards's approach pretty well pegged. "You know, when you win, that's easy," he says. "But if things go bad, Herman doesn't point the fingers at anybody. He looks at himself first. He's going to keep working. He's not going to dwell on something negative. He's going to pick it up and say, 'Let's keep moving, let's look for the next one. There's something good up ahead. There's something good out there.'"

This idea of having to "cut" players, as Dungy says, is still one of the toughest things to do. However, again, he learned that lesson well. What usually happens when a team cuts you is that you are told, "The head coach wants to see you—and bring your playbook." The "playbook" is the "bible" for each team—formations, stunts, special nuances, etc.—and a head coach confiscates it when a player is cut.

Herm learned an important lesson when he was cut from the Eagles. Dick Vermeil had left the Eagles to take a network-broadcasting job. So the new head coach called Herm in—with his playbook. When he handed over the playbook, the head coach never even looked at him—never looked him in the eye—never said "thanks for the nine years spent with the Eagles." That really hurt, and it took a long time to get over. So today, as head coach, when Herm has to cut a player, he always sits the player down, looks him straight in the eye, explains the decision, and points out that other opportunities—in and out of football—will come his way. Coach Edwards wishes him well and leaves the door open for him to call if he can ever help. It's still difficult. It never becomes routine.

When Herm considers all of the good direction and guidance he has received from all the people he has been privileged enough to be exposed to, he thinks about the lesson beyond the lesson of the moment. When the teaching and coaching was at its best, he picked up some important lessons concerning a specific situation, but there was always something more. There was always the implication of something deeper. The best teachers always probed toward a virtue that defies strict definition but signifies a sense of order and purpose, of things being under control. You can call it bedrock serenity, an underlying notion that remaining poised is the only logical reaction to a difficult situation.

Viewed this way, winning and losing are then mere results. One or the other cannot redefine the effort that preceded it. The effort is what it is. It has its own integrity. If it was the best effort going in, it will remain so. The flicker of points on the board won't change that, any more than the atmospheric pressure and relative humidity will decide the spot where a fly ball will land, or the number of qualified applicants showing up to interview for the same job. The effort is what it is. The outcome is sometimes strictly a matter of chance.

Overcoming obstacles, wherever we encounter them in life, can be distilled to the basic formula expressed by Coach Tony Dungy: "It's still a beginning for you." Herm had to hold on to this principle at an early age, pitting himself against the bigger, older, and more experienced pick-up basketball players in Monterey. Swatted down and batted around, he'd keep coming back for more, motivated by a desire to simply take his place among the better players, and encouraged by the words of his father. All he ever wanted was an opportunity. His attitude was "Just show me an opportunity. I'll work for it. Just give me a chance." That's all he ever wanted. And that's the message he got from his dad, who said, "You don't want anyone to give you anything, son. The worst thing people can do is deny you the opportunity to earn it yourself." The next level of understanding those words was to be ready to take advantage of the opportunity when it came. You never know when it's going to come, but you know it will. When you believe and when you prepare, you just know it will.

One practice day with the Eagles coach Vermeil was really testing Herm at corner. Vermeil had his offense run pass play after pass play right at Herm. Coach was "carping"—his way of challenging—testing Herm's mettle. But No. 46 kept his cool and continued to intercept one pass after the other. Tempers were rising. On one final interception Herm ran by Coach Vermeil and spiked the ball, saying, "Keep 'em comin', Coach. I'll be ready!" Coach laughed and patted him on the back. They bonded a friendship then and there that has never wavered.

Here the formula becomes even more simplified. Never giving up, refusing to quit, staying the course, hanging in there, toughing it out, fighting the good fight—these are all shorthand mottoes for preserving opportunity. It simply becomes the business we have to take care of in order to stand ready when the chance comes. The setbacks to any plan should be seen as secondary concerns, as elements that should not cause the vision of one's opportunity to waver. Nothing is absolute. You know that when you're going through the difficulties. There are going to be some bumps in the road, and you're going to hit a few of them. What you have to concentrate on is the big picture. The little bumps are going to happen but the big picture is still there. You fall down, and you get right back up. There it is, the big picture. But you won't see it, if your head's not held up.

In the NFL, the post-game press opportunity is often as great a test of a coach's character as anything he does on the field. Here he needs to tell the truth and sustain the vision simultaneously, and anyone who has ever attempted to do this—especially after an unexpected or humiliating loss—can confirm how difficult a chore it is. The coach needs to remain upbeat, but not in a Pollyannaish sort of way. The hokum detectors are finely tuned in the world of football, from the owners, to the players, to the beat writers, and right on down to the fans. The chief needs to be informative, but not to the point of revealing privileged information. He can be critical, but he must always gauge the potential effect of his words on his team's trust. When he's done saying his piece, the last thing a coach needs to feel is regret—either for something he said, or for something he didn't say.

The following is a chronological look at how Coach Edwards

used that forum and attempted to work on the big picture during the 2002 season:

On April 28, 2002 Coach Edwards declared, "Vinny Testaverde is our starting quarterback and we all know that. I expect him to have a fantastic year, as well as our football team."

On September 10, after the Jets' opening win against the Buffalo Bills in overtime, Herm said, "These guys truly expected to win. They really did. There is a sense with these guys that they are going to get it done."

On September 17, the questions were blunt after a staggering loss in New England to the Patriots. "What are we?" he inquired of the reporters. "Right now, when I watch us play, I really don't know what we are. I kind of watch us and we do a little bit of this and do a little bit of that. Last year, we had an identity . . . Now we have to define what we are going to be."

The team fell to 1-2 after another lopsided loss, this time to the Miami Dolphins on September 22, prompting this comment, "I think everyone is frustrated right now—the whole football team. Everyone is searching for answers, trying to know what to do. You just have to go to work, keep working on the little things, and do it better. What will get the players' confidence back? Winning a game."

On September 30, after the Jets' fourth loss in Jacksonville to the Jaguars, Coach Edwards made news across the country by replacing veteran starting quarterback Vinny Testaverde with Chad Pennington, a third-year man who had never started a game for the club. "It's not all on Vinny," he said, "but the quarterback takes the first hit. It is a gut feeling. What we have to do is get a spark going, and I think we just have to go this way at this point." The move did not bring instant success the following week against the Kansas City Chiefs, but the improvement justified the decision to make the change. Chad spoke for the entire organization when he pointed out that "Sunday's game was an event full of reason to believe. They [the fans] saw a different team out there with a different type of attitude. Now we just have to get over the hump, and once we get over the hump, we will definitely have even more reason to believe." In a press conference that week with the Jets now 1-4, a reporter asked about something sort of "writing the season off" now with four losses. Coach Edwards bristled, and although his remarks were pointed he kept his composure. "Write off the season! Quit? Not on my watch," he fired back. Then he continued, "You play to win the game"—and looked right at the reporter who was writing, "Hello?" Herm said "You play to win the game."

A win against the Minnesota Vikings and a loss to the Cleveland Browns brought a 2-5 Jets team to San Diego and a packed house backing the streaking 6-1 Chargers. A subdued atmosphere in the Jets' clubhouse prior to the game gave no hint of the wrecking ball that had been smuggled into it. Snickering attention had been paid to the team for its now-you see-' em, now-you-don't quality in the early season. This prompted the rhetorical question, "They are saying they don't think we have a chance. Who in this locker room doesn't think we have a chance?" Herm said to the team. They answered his question with an unrhetorical score of 44-13.

On November 10 a rejuvenated Jets club hosted the Miami Dolphins and won with a John Hall field goal in the closing minutes. The post-game press conference was short and to the point in appraising the performance in that game. "We talked all week about how, when the opportunity opens, we have to take advantage of it," Herm said. "I thought we did that as a football team tonight."

Additional wins against the Detroit Lions and the Buffalo Bills resurrected hopes for a respectable season, if not a guaranteed run at the playoffs. Credit for the changing fortunes was spread all around the organization, but a more generous share was given, deservedly, to the remarkably poised young quarterback Pennington. No one was more supportive of his starter role than Testaverde, the man he replaced, but it was as clear as the biblical passage from Ecclesiastes that Pennington's time had come. It was a pleasure for Herm to be able to restate one of his foundation principles as he described the success that Pennington was experiencing. "Chad has prepared himself [to be successful]." He said. "When you prepare yourself and surround yourself with players who are fulfilling their roles, it makes your role a lot easier. This is how he has gone about his business and how he is running this football team right now. It is good for him and it is good for the guys that are around him. They are playing a lot better right now."

There is no such thing as a trail up a steep slope that contains no loose footing, and the Jets slipped on it in Oakland during a Monday Night game against the Raiders. Coach tried not to sing the blues or pump sugar water over the loss that brought the team to 6-6. Instead he daubed at the big picture with simple observations. "Every game—we play to win," he said. "We felt that way after the bye. Every time we played a game, it was important for us to win. That's been our mindset all the way. We didn't think about the whole season, we just thought about each game—one game at a time. There's no margin for error anymore. When you get to six losses, it's tough. You need to win. You definitely need to win. We know that. We've been playing like that for the last five weeks."

A 19-13 win over the Denver Broncos lent a prophetic air to his comments from the previous week, and stimulated a similar response as the Jets prepared for their final three games. There was no room left for anything but the best football this group of players could produce, and Coach was as forthright as possible in relaying this fact. "We have to have a mindset that we're not that good of a football team to think we can go up there (Chicago) and not function well," he said. "We have to function well. We're not good enough not to. We're really not."

The Jets then proceeded to lose to the Bears in Chicago, and the season's momentum took another baffling pause. Since it falls to the head coach to be the hands-on manager of his team's attitude, Herm sifted through the aftermath and held it up for honest inspection. He told the press, "After a loss like that, you try and rejuice the batteries. We played so well for six weeks. All of a sudden, where did this come from? That's what hurts. I didn't anticipate it. It's a shame that we didn't play to our level. We let the Bears hang around and tried to win it at the end. Right now our focus is just on winning our next game and getting things going again. It's not unrealistic. That's what I've continued to remind the players . . . As I've said the last four weeks, we're a team with a lot of anxiety. That brings out two things. Either you get scared and can't play or you get focused. We're pretty focused."

In order to keep the team focused on where they were headed, he made the decision not to show the Bears game film to the players. On Mondays, if the Jets lose, they have a team meeting; stretching and light work out—mandatory. The coaches don't want the players deciding for themselves why we lost. They want to set the direction and keep everyone on the same page—to maintain focus. Showing their poor performance to the players would only create doubt and confusion. Focus to win was Herm's message. To this day, the Jets players have not seen that game film.

The Jets' trip to New England for the return date with the Patriots on December 22 wound up bearing unlikely playoff implications. The Jets, of course, had to win, and when they dispatched the defending NFL champs by a score of 30-17, the division title was still up for grabs. The press conferences that week were full of enthusiasm for the next challenge. Edwards reminded the team, "When we went out to San Diego in November, we were 2-5, and the Chargers were 6-1. Now, with one game left, we have the same record. It would be an unbelievable story if we make the playoff." The Patriots' game was like a playoff game. If they lost, they were out. It was very intense. They had spent a lot of energy getting back into the race. It was a high anxiety ride. But they developed a sense of "this is how it is. We don't know any better. We have to get through it. We have to finish it."

With fate dangling, the Jets hosted the Green Bay Packers for the regular season finale on December 29, and just as predicted and hoped for, a football game broke out and "Gang Green" sat with a four-point lead at the half. The Jets had their heads down at halftime, so Coach called upon them and told them they were going to win the game. "Don't have your heads down. It is going to be tough, but we are going to win the game," he challenged them. The Jets returned to the field and, whether emotionally charged or secretly hypnotized, outscored the Packers by a margin of twenty-one points in the second half. When the Miami Dolphins lost to the New England Patriots earlier that same afternoon (it was a late afternoon game with the Packers), the crowd erupted. The Jets offense poured it on and at the end of game was into the postseason for a second consecutive year, winning the division for the second time in club history. Receiver Laveranues Coles lifted a bright page out of the team handbook when he proclaimed after the game, "You have to believe in yourself. No matter what anybody says about you or thinks about you, you have to believe in yourself."

Belief was running high when the Meadowlands filled to overflowing for the first round playoff game against the Indianapolis Colts on January 4, 2003, and Herm was facing his good friend and mentor Tony Dungy, now the Colts' head coach. A strategic convergence in the stadium that day bundled all elements of the Jets' organization into a tight package, and Indianapolis never figured out how to open it. The final score was 41-0. You can never get too self-satisfied after a blowout; you never know when you might be on the other side of the loop. "They just caught us on a good day" was Herm's post-game comment. "We were firing on all cylinders." The team was also talking on all open mikes, and each standing spokesman represented the Jets' achievement in words that echoed the coaching staff's consistent vision for the team. "This just goes to show you what can happen when a team pulls together," fullback Richie Anderson said. "I think we have proven, especially in this season, anything can happen." Chad Pennington added, "I am so proud of the way the guys came together. But I am also really proud that we are not satisfied."

Seeking the opportunity for further "dissatisfaction," the Jets fell flat in the second round, losing 30-10 to an Oakland Raiders club that felt it had been overlooked and disrespected in the midst of the media blitz directed at us during the early playoffs. (The Raiders went on to play in Super Bowl XXVII but lost to Tampa Bay.) Pennington was mauled early and often by an aggressive Raiders defense that took away his favored medium-range pass routes on crossing patterns and forced him to throw deep and wide against his better judgment, resulting in uncharacteristic turnovers. The quarterback's and the team's rhythm were misplaced and never recovered. The halftime "failure management" course didn't produce an answer on January 12. And so the campaign ended, beyond the boundaries of what conventional wisdom had dictated for the Jets, but short of our goal of one more win.

As Herm led his team through that lurching second season, he was always mindful of focusing attention on the "big picture" that was a short bridge away from the immediate success or crisis. In coaching vocabulary, "staying on course" is not always just a momentary grab for courage but rather a collection of tests spread over the course of a schedule. Beneath them all it is the coach's guidance that is a consistent and dependable presence. His public statements were meant to be the hum from the engine room below decks, encouraging his players to drive on.

In any such collection of tests, whether it is an athletic season, a scholastic course, an illness, a marriage, or a childrearing, consistent stature in the face of conflict, controversy, and disappointment is not to be hoped for but rather to be lived. As a certain influential man told Herm a long time ago, "Never let 'em see you sweat, and never let anybody steal your grin." Herm lives his life that way. No matter how bad it ever gets, they're not going to steal his grin. He's built that way, and he fortifies that characteristic with his personal discipline and development. That's how he views life. When they can start robbing you of your grin, they affect you internally, and you can't let that happen. In the world Coach Edwards represents, never giving up is always about the search for one more opportunity, one more chance to show how well you have prepared.

CHAPTER 2

A Quick Lap Around
The History Track

The attraction of a career American soldier to a German girl working in the PX at a base in Gelhausen after WWII began the romance that took its time developing. After six years, Herman Edwards Sr., and Martha Gerstner were ready for a lifetime commitment. They married in Germany in February 1953 and returned to the United States a couple of months later, Herman Sr. reporting for duty at Fort Monmouth in New Jersey. It was a simple life, revolving around the institutional give and take that existed between the U.S. Army and one of its sergeants, with one complicating factor: he was an African-American, and his new bride was a white woman of German descent. "Ed," as his friends called Herman Sr. was born in Tupolo, Mississippi, the youngest of three children. His family moved to Memphis where he grew up. Martha, just a teenager when World War II started, grew up in Germany and had to endure the bombings and strafing of American aircraft as she tried to understand what that war was all about.

In Germany, the unconventional racial pairing was somewhat insulated by both military culture and the need for Germany to atone for its staggering record of persecution. Still, her parents were deeply worried about their daughter's prospects. She was not only leaving home; she was leaving her country, and its continent as well. The fact that she was marrying a black man was more of an unspoken apprehension, but it added to their anxiety in a world of unknowns. In the United States, such a marriage at that time was rare and tolerated only in small circles. The army was one of those. While Herman and Martha were waiting for housing on the base at Fort Monmouth to open up, they moved into a temporary place in town.

Martha recalls, "We had to rent, and we rented from a black lady who was very nice. But there was a house directly across the street where some other black women would gather. One day I was hanging out my clothes to dry and these women began yelling at me, saying that I had come over from Germany and stolen one of their men, and that I should go back there. They said that I didn't belong here. I was so upset that I went into the house and cried. When my husband came home I told him 'I want to go back home. I can't stay here. I can't live this way.'"

It was an ungracious welcome, but the intervention of a landlady in making sure such harassment did not recur helped calm Martha's nervousness about her new life in America. Shortly thereafter a woman working in a furniture store, Rose Fisher, befriended her and, after helping her furnish their new base quarters became a warm and helpful presence in Martha's life. "That lady came to our place, met my husband, and never batted an eye—much less anything else," Martha remembers with admiration. "We became best friends. She took me everywhere I wanted to go. She took me to meet all her friends and relatives and told them that I was a distant cousin from Germany. We went to New York. This lady took me everywhere. When Herman was born, well, she just loved Herman." Rose Fisher was a valued friend to the Edwards family.

Herman was born on April 27, 1954 in Ft. Monmouth, New Jersey. The apfel of his mother's eye—she tells him and that he remains so to this day. Herman was their first contribution to the baby boom. The young family remained in New Jersey until Herman Sr. was transferred back to Germany in 1956, where he was stationed at Nellingan, outside Stuttgart. Herman Jr.'s sister Irvina joined the family in 1958, and the "boom" was officially over in the Edwards household. Geographic uncertainty is not a great stimulus for creating large families, and the two-plus-two lineup enabled the family to stay flexible.

Which was a good thing, since the army was not done moving Herman Sr. around. In 1959 they were back in the U.S., this time Herman's dad reporting to Fort Ord in Seaside, California. They played the same game of housing roulette in California that they had played in New Jersey, living off the base until government housing became available. But a twist was added in 1961 when the master sergeant received orders for a transfer to Korea, which meant that his family would have to vacate their quarters on the base. So they decided to buy a house in Seaside, where Martha would live with Herman and Irvina while their dad was satisfying his one-year obligation in Asia. Thus a pattern was established. Herman Sr. would venture out on military assignment as a master sergeant, or later, following his retirement from the army, to where his jobs as a construction foreman led him, usually somewhere in the San Jose Area. Back in Seaside, Martha managed the household and supervised the day-to-day rearing of the children.

Irvina, now married with a boy Joshua and a daughter Tamika, is one of the prettiest women in the universe. Tamika, her daughter, recently received an award for her "motivation, volunteerism and outstanding character." Those traits seemed to be handed down from her grandparents.

Seaside was an open, spirited place where everyone was welcome, and as Herman grew older the neighborhood became a hub of youth activity in this small town. In particular, his home became a nucleus of male energy that he stirred up daily by bringing his friends over to hang out in the garage that his dad had painstakingly converted into a recreation room. His mom gave Herman the nickname of "Bobie" (German slang for "pretty boy") so she would say, "When Bobie and his buddies were not cleaning out my larder they could generally be found flinging one ball or another at the local Boys Club."

This was a shack-like oasis that provided the local kids with the minimum equipment required for competing with each other. (The dilapidated early building has since been rebuilt, the result of a campaign Herm orchestrated later on (see Chapter 8).

The times, they were a-changin', and America was shifting from the placid tone of the post-war '50s to the turbulence of the '60s, when "Bobie" found his grip on a broomstick that quiet but fateful morning. He stood at the brink of a decade that would shake the foundations of American cultural institutions, but there was a steadiness that characterized life in the Edwards family, an orientation toward order rather than chaos that allowed his youthful energy to develop freely but with great discipline.

This may be attributed in no small measure to his dad's deeply held belief in work, personal responsibility, and upholding the dignity of one's name. Working full time from the age of fourteen, his dad found in the army an environment where lack of education wouldn't matter and tireless attention to detail would be rewarded. This had a profound effect on his son and was the basis of a relationship that deepened through the years. Herman Sr. was a very humble and hardworking man. He taught his son very early on to respect what he did as a person. Herman Sr. was a mechanic in the service, and he talked about details, and doing the right thing and knowing your job. It wasn't just doing things right, it was recognizing the correct thing to do. Herman Jr. can remember when they would be driving early in the morning near the base, and reveille would play over the outdoor speakers. Dad would stop the car and say, "Get out, son, we've got to look to the east." And they would look toward where the flag was and salute. Nobody would see them if they didn't, but they would know.

Herm stated his faith in his father this way, "I always knew where I stood with him. He was the kind of dad who would let me make a decision and live with it as I got older, but only after he helped me prepare for it. He would paint the picture and then stand back quietly and say 'Okay, what do you want to do?' Disciplined freedom was what he encouraged, and this message resonated in me." The steadiness, the quiet certainty that things would follow a correct course, was a vital component of his father's character, and it was passed on to a son now discovering the depths of the gift.

As a young boy, Herm would watch his father get up early on Saturday mornings and go out to carefully sweep the driveway and sidewalk before washing Martha's car. It was a ritual followed with a pilgrim's devotion, even after he retired from the army and went into the construction business. Even though there were many weeks when that job kept him away from home until Friday night, his sweeping and scrubbing on Saturday morning announced his return and reconfirmed his commitment to the home life he shared with his family. In junior high, Herm began to absorb some of the responsibility for the good appearance of his mother's car and the front of the house, and the Saturday cleaning became one of his regular chores. After his dad's death in 1978, when Herm would return to Seaside during the NFL off season, he found himself sweeping the same stretch of pavement with a nearly unconscious regularity, grabbing a broom every couple of days and paying tribute to his dad. He still does it. His mom would often ask, "What are you doing?" during his frequent visits to the old house, hoping he wouldn't feel that such zealous cleanliness is something he owes her. Herman would say, "I'm just sweeping."

The steadiness in Edwards was also the result of the relationship between his dad and mom, whose unconventional marriage required an abiding love and strength of character to flourish. "You've got to understand," Edwards says, "My mom left her family in Germany. They didn't want her to marry 'Ed' in the first place. And then to come all the way to America—you're talking about the '50s now—that was a tough hurdle. You just don't do that." That's why Herman gives his mom credit. She really loved "Ed." For a woman to give up the security of one life for the total unknown of another, and to go . . . words fall short of the respect and affection that Herman has for his mother.

Martha remembers only a single time when Herman asked about the obvious physical differences between them. She explained that it was simply God's design, and then she quickly asked if he had a problem, fearing that he had discovered too early the pain of ridicule and exclusion. Herman said, "No, I just wanted to know." Even at a young age, Herman exhibited a somewhat mature awareness of that unusual racial status, and seemed to understand that genetic melding provided a unique perspective and opportunity. His singular identity as a man with blood citizenship in both the African-American and white cultures was an instrument of cohesion rather than division, and seemed to provide a strength that he has never shied from.

In growing up Herm made a conscious decision to play, work, and study hard. He was a buoyant kid who was constantly smiling, moving, and wrapping his world into a bundle of banter that he used to sell himself and motivate the people around him. Herm saw profit in shining servicemen's shoes at Fort Ord, for thirty-five cents, thus sparing our soldiers the chore of polishing their own. And for a dollar he would liberate a homeowner from the necessity of mowing his lawn. When he wasn't being a walking entrepreneur, he found dishwashing jobs on the base and built a budget around that minimum wage. At home, he performed assigned chores with no prompting, just figuring out what needed to be done to help and just doing it. Martha speaks of Herman with the sort of awe found in a person trying to recall a

UFO encounter. She's aware that it defies logic and the conventional wisdom about boys at that age, but since she did observe it with her own eyes, she holds fast to her account.

His first team athletic experience was playing Pony League baseball at age ten in Seaside, for a coach named Jim Cota who recognized Herm's strengths and abilities. The results of all the games are a blur, buried as they are by the fruitful lives and careers of both of them at higher levels of achievement. But Jim Cota, who remains a close friend, has a distinct memory of what could be described as Coach Edwards's "early coaching style," the one that he probably began practicing as soon as he put on a uniform. "Herman always felt the need to motivate the other guys," Cota recalls. "He would talk to them about how important this game was, how we take it one game at a time. Then during the game, he'd sit in the dugout with our pitcher Paul Joyce, who was a top-notch pitcher, a big kid who threw BBs but who got really wound up emotionally as he was overwhelming our opponents. Herman would calm him down, slow him down, and make him take it easy."

"He did that with a lot of players," Cota tells people. "Herman would just go sit with them and talk to them, especially during the bad times. I can still hear Herman saying 'There's a reason for everything.' I don't know if he was coaching, or if he was just trying to bring the best out of these kids. Maybe there's not a difference. But he just wanted to do what he could to bring out the best in people." Cota says, "This was not typical of a ten-year-old kid playing in his first baseball league."

Herm is most commonly remembered by boldly declaring his belief in himself and those around him. His first appearance as a high school football player illustrates another facet of that inexhaustible self-expression, when he attended Highland Elementary School in Seaside, then moved on to MLK Junior High. By the time he was ready to begin high school in tenth grade, desegregation had created a bussing program on the Monterey Peninsula. The Edwards's house lay, by happenstance, in a zone claimed by Monterey High School, and so he was bussed there while many of the kids in that neighborhood went to Seaside High School. As a new sophomore, he came face to face with Coach Dan Albert (who later was Mayor of Monterey for 20 years) for the first time during a team meeting.

"It's an orientation about the whole program," recollects Albert.

"There's this school-pride thing, the winning thing, and all that. It got so that I could do that speech pretty well, because it was the same sermon. Basically, we were winning, and we wanted to keep that going. Well, as I was talking it was pretty quiet, except for one guy in the back of the room. I'd stop and say, 'Who's that talking?' and then I'd start again. Pretty soon he'd start again. After a few shots at it I said, 'Wait a minute. What's your name back there?' And he said, "My name is Herman Edwards, Sir; but you can call me 'Mr. Bob.'"

"Mr. Bob," Bob Hayes, was his absolute idol. "It was all I could do to keep from laughing," said Coach Albert, "because it was just one of those moments—he wasn't being smart. I mean, I asked him a question and he gave me the answer without hesitation. He was a confident young man but not arrogant. I wouldn't ever use the word arrogant about Herman. Afterward, the other coaches and I talked about it and we just roared laughing. That was my introduction to Herman. And then, what we decided to do was to keep him on the squad. He was one of about seven sophomores we kept on the varsity that year—a real change of policy for us. You could see Herman had tremendous ability. Not enough to play a lot that year, but that was because he didn't have any experience at any lower level of playing football."

By his junior year, Herm was a starting safety on the Monterey High School varsity, and any lack of experience was banished to the realm of the irrelevant. He answered to "Mr. Bob" until Hayes fell out of favor with the law, and "Bobie" seemed to be behind for good—with the notable exception of Martha and a small circle of intimate friends, who to this day still call him "Bobie." However, as Herman progressed on the team, the good name so proudly given by his father was surging to the fore. He was proud to be Herman Edwards, his father's son. Herman knew he would always make his dad proud. At the conclusion of his high school experience he had become a local legend on the football field. As a defensive back Herman intercepted twenty-two passes as a junior and nineteen passes in his senior year, which still stands as a high school record. The good name of Herman Edwards was actively pursued by no less than Stanford, Oregon, California, UCLA, Notre Dame, Ohio State, and USC. He accepted a full athletic scholarship for the fall of 1972 from Cal (University of California at Berkley), just a two-hour drive from the family home in Seaside.

He attended Cal for the fall academic year playing on the varsity football team as a freshman. It turned out to be a watershed season as he made the All Pac-8 Team, led the team in interceptions as a safety and set a school record for the most "picks"—four—in a single game. However, strong differences in basic points of view developed between a position coach and Herman who then discussed it with Head Coach Mike White and defensive backfield coach Jim Erkenbeck. After much consideration, Herm felt his personal ethics would be compromised, so he decided to leave Cal. His grand plan for college had turned into an odyssey of disappointment.

Returning home to Seaside, and enrolling at Monterey Peninsula College, a two-year community college, Herm pursued an associate degree. Coaches Luke Phillips and Chris Pappas had wanted him to come there straight out of Monterey High. They helped turn Herman's disappointment into a fresh opportunity by switching him from safety to cornerback. He found a home at that position—one that he never strayed from for the rest of his playing days. He met his educational goals and played for a fine MPC team whose nickname is the Lobos. Herm was determined to make his mark as the best Lobo ever, and he did (Herman was elected to the Lobo Hall of Fame in 1991). After a strong season at MPC, he enrolled at San Diego State without the benefit of a scholarship. To pay his way through school, he worked nights at a shipyard.

In his second season at San Diego State he was granted an athletic scholarship, starting at corner on a team that went 10-1 during the 1976 season. Under the tutelage of Claude Gilbert and future NFL coach Ernie Zampese, he earned a spot in the Hula Bowl as a college all-star that year, which might have had something to do with his pulsating visibility on teams from major football programs. Although he performed very well in his final year of college football, and despite what he hoped, Herm was not taken in the NFL draft in the spring of 1977. The dream of playing professional football that he had verbally guaranteed in every kitchen where he had washed a dish at Fort Ord was momentarily shot down with uncertainty.

The 1977 draft had not been completed for very long before Herm's phone started to ring, as the Dolphins, the Giants, the Raiders, and the Eagles all figured they could tilt the can and find the "bonus," that everybody else missed. Don Shula, head coach of the Miami Dolphins, made the most persuasive case, and the next day,

Herm entered the rarefied world of "Can you be here tomorrow? We want to take a look at you," as Shula puts it. Herm flew to Miami and worked out for two days as a free agent. In checking phone messages being saved by a friend in San Diego, he discovered that Carl Peterson, formerly of UCLA, then a coach at Philadelphia, and now the president of the Kansas City Chiefs, had called to make a pitch for the Eagles. Peterson established enough of a rapport to extract a promise from Herm that he wouldn't sign with anybody else until the Eagles had a chance to work him out. Herm agreed.

The next day, Herm, still working out with the Dolphins, was getting ready to leave, when Don, Mr. Shula, brings him in with Bobby (Beathard) and they're saying, "You're the only guy here who hasn't signed with us yet, and we want you to sign." Bobby was saying, "Hey, you've got an excellent chance of making this football team and you're going to be a good player in this league."

Herm said, "Well, you know, I'd like to sign, but I can't. I gave my word to the Eagles that I'd go visit them."

Coach Shula said, "You can't do that!"

But Herm, who keeps his promises, said, "I've got to go there, I gave my word." And he did, getting on a plane in Miami and flying all the way to Los Angeles. He got off one plane in L.A. and on another one straight to San Diego. Carl Peterson is waiting for Herm at the airport. They get in a car and drive back to L.A.; they got on a midnight flight and flew to Philadelphia. The next day Herm was at the Eagles camp, a mini camp for their draft choices, and started working out with them the next day.

Herm signed with the Eagles, led in 1977 by Dick Vermeil, with whom he developed a close relationship over the course of nine years in Philadelphia. As for the snaring of this "unheralded cornerback" from San Diego State, Peterson observes in pleased retrospect, "I thought Herman was the best college free agent out there. I was right and Bobby Beathard didn't move fast enough."

Martha attests to the jubilation that seized the Fort Ord kitchens when word got around about Herman making it to the NFL. It was slightly muted at home—not that the family wasn't proud. But his dad had not been an athlete himself, and when his son was playing football in high school, Master Sergeant Edwards was serving his country in Korea. After returning and retiring from the army, "Ed's" construction work kept him away during the weeknights when football ruled male consciousness, so he was an infrequent spectator at best during his son's developing high school and college career. Whether his dad would have evolved into a more enthusiastic follower of the game can only remain a matter of speculation. During Herman's first season with the Eagles, his dad died of injuries sustained when he lost control of the company truck he was driving and crashed. It was later discovered that his dad had diabetes, which he kept secret from his family and friends. The truck accident was a result of his fainting (possibly hypoglycemic shock due to low blood sugar) and thus losing consciousness. It was a difficult loss for anyone who had ever been on the receiving end of Ed's decency as a person, and all the more so for the family that loved him and owed so much to his hard work and sacrifice.

Herm Edwards's NFL career lasted for ten years, nine spent in Philadelphia and the final season split between the Los Angeles Rams and the Atlanta Falcons. When the Rams released him after the second week of the 1986 season, his old coach from the Eagles, Marion Campbell called. Campbell, who was now head coach at the Atlanta Falcons, said, "Herm, come to Atlanta. We have a place for you here." When he arrived at the Falcons camp, a huge sign was in the locker room: "Welcome Herm Edwards." Coach Campbell wanted Herman not only to feel welcome but also to let others know the contribution Herman can make to a team.

"Herm was one of the prototypical overachievers," recalls Ron Jaworski, the former Eagle quarterback-turned-broadcaster. "He had limited speed, good size, but the system was right for him. It was a system that required intelligence and discipline, and that's really what his game was as a player. Tremendous discipline. He knew how to read the quarterback as well as the wide receivers. He read the triangle, played the game, and probably played longer than his God-given talent. He shouldn't have played that long. He wasn't that good. And I don't mean that in a negative way at all. They just could never get rid of him because he was such a fierce competitor. He loved to play, and he knew his strengths and weaknesses."

The only one who could make Herm go away was himself, and so he recognized his time to move on at the end of the 1986 season. He reached for "the broom" once again. That hybrid philosophy of advanced self-confidence and a better world through sport—the best in him bringing out the best in the game/society/world around him—

has become an institution within the large heart and fierce determination. Jim Erkenbeck observes, "Herman could have headed the other way. This guy could have failed, easily. All the characteristics indicated that he could have failed. Mixed marriage, isolated community, father dies early, mother speaking with broken English. You can build a case for a guy who could be robbing 7-elevens."

Except that Herm wasn't going to let that happen. He had more important things to do, like doing what he had been doing all along, even as a player: coaching. It was a natural transition. It followed the standard of correctness, of one thing leading doubtlessly to the next that his father had instilled in him. "Yeah, well, he's a coach," observes Carl Peterson when informed that his call for Herm to come work on an NFL coaching staff had prevented him from taking a scheduled job at Jim Cota's van and storage company in Monterey. "You can just tell that about certain people," Peterson concluded.

So Herm began his NFL coaching adventure with the Kansas City Chiefs working on their staff through the NFL's Intern Program in 1989. (See chapter 9 for more on the NFL Intern Program.)

CHAPTER 3

Keeping Time

I think Herman has three simple rules. One is like, "Be on time." The other is "Be professional." And the third one . . . I can't remember the third one.

—Joe Bommarito

It's not fuzzy headedness that caused Herm's longtime friend Joe Bommarito to misplace the third concept. Rather, it's his wise recognition of the importance of the first two that renders the forgotten one to nearly irrelevant status. Of course, when Joe finally succeeds in recalling it, he'll give himself one of those smacks in the head that usually accompanies a line like, "How could I have forgotten that?" But he needn't be too hard on himself. The notions of being on time and being a professional are wide-ranging and all-inclusive. If you get those two right, chances are very good that everything else will take care of itself, or at least be highly clarified along the way.

These points are strongly reinforced throughout the New York Jets players' playbook, beginning with the first item listed under "Expectations for Training Camp and Regular Season Policies." The playbook is the fifty-page statement of values and purpose that covers everything beyond the Xs and Os of the playbook, and it bears Edwards's imprint as the coach whose organization produced it. The NFL includes all of its regulations and mandates, but as the head coach, Herm gets in the first word and that sets the tone for the material to follow. He jumped at the opportunity to be the leader of the Jets, because setting the tone boiled down to delivering a simple and unerring instruction about winning. So there in the Jets' bible, underlined in uppercase bold letters, appears Herm's command that all new and returning professional football players must follow: *BE ON TIME!*

45

But what exactly does it mean to "be on time"? One needs to probe beneath the obvious reference to the hands of the clock to gather in the full influence of the phrase, though we're all aware that sometimes the hands of the clock tell the whole story. A lineman hazy on the snap count may cost his team a first down, a touchdown, or a playoff berth. Anybody showing up at 11:01 for the 11:00 ferry at a dock where the boats are running on time will likely remain a landlubber. A conference call that has to loiter past its scheduled start time waiting for participants to check in is going to penalize somebody's budget. And if the timepieces had not been well synchronized in Houston, not even baby steps would have been taken on the moon by Neil Armstrong and company in 1969. Still, there is an underlying order to the business of time and its management that transcends the clock, and to Herman Edwards it is a nearly sacred principle.

We're not born in a timeless limbo. There is always a sequence, the well-ordered rhythm of life surging toward the moments and experiences that we must encounter simply because we live and breathe. And there are also those moments and experiences that we have created for ourselves, for which we have exercised judgment, choice, and will. Creation rolls along these twin tracks, one supervised by the animating power we name according to our beliefs, the other controlled by our individual recognition of what we want and what we need in any given circumstance. Life and purpose resides in the space between.

Time is imposed on us: witness a family sitting around a campfire on the beach, enjoying the achingly good final moments of a summer vacation they hate to see end but one that they'll never forget. There is the last ride to the vet for a beloved old dog and the retirement dinner for the founder of the preschool. How many of us have driven to one of our own reunions bewildered by the number that was assigned to it, wondering if we're still recognizable as the person we used to be? Consider a sixty-minute football game that is undecided as the two-minute warning is issued, or an order from a soot-streaked firefighter to evacuate before the fire hits the ridge above the house in fifteen minutes. Time may sometimes strike us as being relentless in its advance, unknowable and unbendable, anxious to leave us in its wake. Our response to this constant life pressure may be optimistic or pessimistic, cynical or serene, yet all the best efforts of mankind's imagination have so far failed to defeat it.

But we also keep time on our own, and life is often a challenge to maintain or revive a personal tempo. We work to a beat, beginning with the heart, the elemental drum that can always tell us what time it is. Our personal rhythms find resonance in the world beyond ourselves, in the seasons and cycles that are larger than we are. In the course of a lifetime we have acquired a vast collection of heartbeats and changes, a time signature as distinct as a fingerprint, a drumbeat that has supplied the cadence for our time here.

However we orient ourselves to the mystery of passing time, the fact remains that it simply does. This is both humbling and ennobling. Humbling, because we are utterly powerless over it. We can't escape nature's deadlines, and we can't argue with the constant passage of the present into the past. Only in the vivid human imagination do we find the means by which we can slow down, stop, or reverse time. Making time "stand still" is the benchmark quality of a good romance, or, for that matter, any human experience that fully engages our emotions. Nostalgia is the formal name for this quest, and it is the rare individual who hasn't experienced it. It has an unusual power over humans because it encourages us to experience what is known and familiar in a world full of change and uncertainty, and can provide a pleasant escape or time out from the conditions we can't control. Of course, the more time we spend looking backward in search of life's satisfaction, the more likely we are to distort the reality of our previous experience, but that is a risk many people are quite at home with.

The passage of time is ennobling because it makes us finite, and it gives us a brief opportunity to express ourselves. Time is always running out or running away; how do we make the best use of it? That question is the constant companion of all human endeavors. "Nobody gets out of here alive," goes the philosophical joke. Eternal life is a spiritual matter; our physical time is here and now. What can we make of it?

Coach Edwards often asks the kids at The Youth Foundation camp each June in Monterey, "How many of you want to go to heaven?" Without exception each of those eight-hundred-plus kids, ages nine to eighteen, raises his hand. Then he asks, "Okay, so you all want to go to heaven, how many of you want to die?" No hands. "Well, everyone wants to go to heaven, but nobody wants to die, how ya gonna get there?" Then there is a long pause.

Coach continues, "I understand, I don't want to die either, at least not now, but I will. And when the time comes, I'll be ready." What's important in these questions is that each of us must sacrifice something to get what we want. Often we must sacrifice something to be on time. You've got to make it a priority, and unless you do, you'll not be on time and others will have to sacrifice their time to wait for you.

The obvious in this current of passing time is the opportunity to be prepared. Edwards believes strongly in the power of the arriving moment, when we have the chance to do something right or meaningful with the opportunity we have been presented.

A foundation of his coaching philosophy is that when preparation is complete, the right results will follow.

"What I see in this current of passing time is the opportunity to be prepared," says Edwards. "I believe strongly in the power of the present moment, when we have the chance to do something right or meaningful with the opportunity we have been presented. A foundation of my coaching philosophy is that when preparation is complete, the right results will follow."

"I always tell my players that in their lifetimes they will practice more than they will every play. And so when they get an opportunity to play, I really want them to enjoy that. You really have to embrace those chances. You've got to play when that time arrives. You can't miss that opportunity and lay it off on bad timing, or say, 'Hey, man, I wasn't ready; I wasn't prepared.' Because you only have so many shots at playing." In the world of professional sports there are no allowances made for lack of motivation, planetary imbalances, or bad biorhythms. If you have what it takes you show it, repeatedly and tirelessly. For as long as you have to. Period.

"In my own case, I understood the work that it was going to take and the sacrifices I was going to have to make for the opportunity to be in someone's camp. And believe me, I made a lot of sacrifices. People sometimes think 'Well, he's a good athlete, it just comes to him' and all that, but there were a lot of sacrifices. I'm talking about letting the parties and the nightlife take their proper place in your order of priorities. I'm talking about how you get up in the morning, every morning before dawn, and work out when the other guys aren't working out. I saw guys slip by the wayside and muster too little effort too late to help themselves. But I wanted to make sure that when I got the opportunity to play professional football that I was ready. If I didn't make it, at least I would know that I did everything within my power to get there. I didn't want to have an excuse. To me, that would have been like wearing a scarlet letter. I would have been marked by my lack of resolve."

Ex-Philadelphia Eagles wide receiver Ron Johnson tells a story about his college days, when he would work out at Monterey Peninsula College with his friend LeCharls McDaniel during the NFL's off-season. Coincidentally, that was a time when Herm could often be found making use of the same facilities at MPC, and as Johnson tells it, their paths did cross. Herm was never aware of being observed to the extent that Johnson describes, but that helps prove the point that everything we do, every action we take, has an effect that we should take responsibility for. Herm was just trying to maintain an acceptable level of preparation for his professional duties, not knowing that he was doubling as a teacher in the process.

"We'd be on the track usually by eight o'clock and the first thing we'd do, we'd run this trail that's behind MPC," Johnson recalls. "It's about a three-mile run. We would work pretty hard doing that, and then we would come back, go in the weight room and work out there, and then come back out to the track. And that's where we'd always see Herman. Early in his NFL career, Herman and Herb Lusk, had been running hundreds (one-hundred-yard sprints). They'd run like twelve hundreds straight and then walk back, over and over. And I always thought they kind of acted a little Hollywood. They never really invited LeCharls and me into the workout. They were a little distant with us."

"But anyway," Johnson continues, "we would watch their workouts, and we were saying, 'Well, they don't want to work out with us because they're in the pros already,' and we began to form the opinion that they were big shots and thought that they didn't have to work that hard. They're coming out at nine o'clock and running their hundreds and that was it, while we're running the trail, doing our weights, doing our sprints, and then doing one-on-one drills after that. Then one week we had some other things going on, so we went out to the track earlier in the morning. And there are Edwards and Lusk on the track; they're running quarters, they're running two-hundreds, they're doing all this stuff, they're busting it. And we realized that all those hundreds we saw them running were just the cool down of their workout. They were doing all this stuff in the morning that we never saw."

"We were on one level," Johnson concludes, "and those guys were three levels ahead of us. And that's what finally encouraged us to go up to them and start talking. We didn't know Herman or Herb other than their names and their reputations, but seeing their workout kind of trained me to look at things from a different perspective. We saw the price they were paying to play in that league, to play at that level. Yeah, it was a whole other level."

That's the prioritizing that is being suggested here. It was clear that nothing short of that level of work was going to keep Herm in an NFL uniform, and so nothing got in the way of the work needed to do. During his playing days, he adapted to a state of constant readiness for "the moment," the arrival of his opportunity. It happened every time he laced his shoes for a workout or taped his ankles for a game. Nothing can be taken for granted. Herm was not (to borrow a phrase from the incomparable Muhammad Ali) "the greatest," or "the fastest," or "the prettiest" guy in the game, and so putting in that time was simply what had to be done.

Preparation places elements in a context with each other that allows success to flow from the arrangement like ageless music. Did you ever see Michael Jordan score fifty points? How about a Sandy Koufax's no-hitter? Tiger Woods earning a green jacket at the Masters? The U.S. Women bringing home soccer's World Cup? None of these feats have been accidental or flukey. Not when they occurred, and never in the replaying.

How we initiate the flow is often a determining factor in our success. Everyone is familiar with the maxim about a great journey beginning with one step. There's a pretty good reason why that particular phrase has reached proverbial status in the motivational universe. His early experience happened with his father, Herman Sr., driving around the army base at Fort Ord, California. It has stayed with him today, it and has become a valuable touchstone in a lifelong effort to honor the concept of being right in time by being right on time.

"Reveille is the bugle call that begins a military day, and it used to be played over speakers that were placed in numerous spots around the base," Herm recalls. "That alarm would find you if you were anywhere on the base and when it did, if you were in the service, your duty was clear. If you were driving, you had to get out of the car, look in the direction of the flag, and salute it. I can remember one time when I was with my dad early in the morning and reveille sounded. My dad stopped the car and said, 'Let's get out, son. We got to get out and look to the east.' At first, I thought my dad was joking, but such a reaction would have been fleeting. There was something penetrating about my father's gaze, and there was plenty of authority in his voice, even for such a brief and quietly spoken command. In short order, I found myself out of the car, my feet on the road looking to the east. To my father, this respectful observation was a necessary first step in any day's proceedings, a correct moment that the remainder of the day might follow with clear direction. I have never forgotten this brief orientation at the side of the road, and I refer to it often."

It is quite likely to be summoned when Edwards is communicating the ideas of "correctness" and "doing the right thing"—either one of which might fill in nicely as the missing number three for Joe Bommarito. When you make a commitment to doing things the right way, you find that all the good stuff is interlocking. One strong concept will stand in for or support another. And like different routes on a roadmap, they'll all help get you where you want to go.

The concept of timing, and how correctness flows out of it, is applicable in virtually any situation. Punctuality, the simple act of showing up on time, may make a stronger first impression than anything we wear or say. When we are kept needlessly waiting, we're liable to unfavorably fill in the blanks on someone we don't know. When an important first "beat" is missed, fine grooming, model diction, and ripe ideas do not get their fullest possible evaluation. Before we even register a first impression, we have caused an opinion to be formed, one that may be long lasting and resistant to new evidence. Did we honor the first obligation that was placed on us? Did we show up on time? The tardy person is working at a disadvantage before even getting started. Aside from starting out on compromised footing in our relationships with the people we need to have on our side, being late is impractical and inefficient. Every moment of our absence from a group effort of some sort is time that cannot be spent communicating about, preparing for, or executing a plan.

Conversely, "staying too long" can upset the rhythm of a quality effort. Coach Edwards is opposed, for instance, to pro players cavorting in the end zone after a touchdown, or prancing around the offensive backfield after a big defensive play. As far as he is concerned, the disrespect shown to fellow professionals is an interruption of the flow of correctness; it is the well-oiled machine bucking and grinding. Watching NFL films of legendary running backs (the names Jim Brown, Gale Sayers, Walter Payton, Barry Sanders and Emmitt Smith come to mind immediately) arriving in the end zone via highly improbable routes, then turning matter-of-factly and freeing the football with a soft flip to the official, is a celebration of its own kind. It acknowledges the job getting done and the paycheck being earned, not the arrival of the circus or the crowning of a king.

"It is a game of respect, and professional players shouldn't belittle each other," Edwards points out emphatically. "I always tell our players, 'If you need to dance, that's fine—but you also need to dance when the other guy catches the ball for a touchdown. If your interception was worth some fancy steps, then let's have it both ways. You let everyone know, hey, he caught the touchdown! I learned a long time ago there's a big piece of humble pie cooked homemade for everybody. You will get your share. It's just a matter of when it gets served to you. If you have not been foolishly trying to advance the world's opinion of you by taunting or disparaging your opponent, you'll find that humble pie goes down a little easier. It's always advisable to spend less time marketing our marvelous qualities and more time fostering those qualities in someone else."

There are other ways to examine the error of overstaying. Not moving on after a defeat falls into this category. If we spend too much time dwelling on a loss, then we dilute the corrective power of learning from our mistakes. Failure to recognize loss and defeat is often a virtual guarantee that we will relive it in a non-constructive way. Grieving—be it over the loss of a loved one, a job, or a game— allows us to move on. A unifying characteristic of people who live to reach the century mark is (along with a sense of humor and a consuming interest in some activity) the ability to handle loss and adjust to a changed world. You see this in the faces of players who linger on the bench, staring out at their victorious opponents rolling and tumbling through a championship celebration. You might wonder if some latent streak of masochism isn't being revealed, for these beaten players to mutely absorb every detail of the frenzy they're not involved in as if it were a train wreck. Far from it. Becoming that intimate with defeat is what allows them to exhale the last of this season's hope, walk slowly back to the clubhouse, and take the first breath of next season's dream. But embracing a setback needs to be time-proportionate. It needs to obey Herman Sr.'s laws of correctness and flow. There is an order to all things, a sequence that speaks itself to us when we pay attention and strive to move ahead with our life's ambitions. Acknowledge and grow. Experience and move on. The loss of Jets Quarterback Chad Pennington serves as a prime example of *experience and move on*. When Pennington broke all the metatarsal bones on his left hand in a preseason game in August, 2003, with rival New York Giants, many fans and some players thought the season might be over, but not Herm Edwards. He now had an opportunity to "walk his talk." And walk he did.

Coach Edwards was upbeat with the players, fans and media. Herm quickly proclaimed his confidence in veteran Quarterback Vinny Testaverde. Herm talked about Vinny's vast experience and how he took the Jets to the playoffs in 1999. Vinny, at age 39, was eager to assume the Jets leadership responsibilities. He never looked at himself as a "backup" but always had it in his head that he was a "starter."

Pennington rose to the occasion as well. He could have felt sorry for himself and written-off the 2003 season. Instead, he was positive and supportive of Vinny. Chad became the Jets number one cheerleader-on the sidelines. The Jets, indeed, were moving on.

Sensing when "our time is up" in a given circumstance is another example. The dilemma of how and when a pro walks away from a playing career is a subject Herm had to take on like so many others have done in the world of professional sport. "The key for me was trusting whatever I had learned about timing. After ten good years and vigorous self-scrutiny, I felt it was time to walk away," he explains. "I felt it deep within me, and I was sure. There was, for me, no agonizing or uncertainty involved in that decision. I probably could have continued playing, but it wasn't in my heart to compete at that level anymore. I resisted the new definition of myself, of course, because the old one was still fresh enough to put on a uniform and play with pride. But I was no longer among the elite at my position, and it was time to try something else."

"The clarity with which I came to at that moment of opportunity was something I'm still grateful for. I didn't want to be a player who took away the opportunity for a younger player to play. It was hard to give it up, but it was in the best interest of the game and my team to start another career. I wanted to coach and another guy was being given a chance to play." Herm's moment would arrive, and he would do something memorable with it. A new moment certainly did arrive, and he's still working hard to fulfill its promise.

One of the principles that Edwards emphasizes with each of the teams he has had the good fortune to coach is the law of showing up. "I can never emphasize strongly enough," he declares. "In fact, each time I communicate how firmly this idea should be worked into our existence as players and people, I reach deeply as I can into myself to make sure the message is fresh and honest. It is so very important. That's what this league—the NFL—is all about. No matter who you are or where you're from, there's something special about you. Of all the guys walking through that clubhouse door, and all the many, many more who aren't walking through that door, there's something unique about each one of them, pure and simple. I tell them not to forget that. You're special. You've got a gift. You've got to use those two things now!," he implores.

"That's part of the deal, because one day that gift they have for playing football is going to leave them," Edwards observes. "Time does its work, age is imposed, skills diminish, and they won't have it anymore—not for the brief chance to shine in the game they want to play. The other opportunities will present themselves, but the performance part of their careers will be over."

It is an inescapable fact of life for a professional athlete, and whether it presents satisfaction or tragedy depends on the outlook of the waning player. The time-sensitive gift to excel in the game of football will have evolved away from its peak, and arguments to the contrary might as well be made to a tall mountain. The coach will begin to look like a more comfortable vantage point from which to observe a game. They may end up as commentators, coaches, or front-office guys. They may sell cars, or real estate, or men's clothes. Some may teach. Others may go back to school. They'll be carried to hundreds of new stations in life, but the one thing they won't be doing is playing professional football.

"To have the gift and not use it is a crying shame," says Edwards. "It may be a delayed realization—you can imagine the man who is sitting in front of the TV with his kids watching a game and talking about what he used to be privileged enough to do for a living. I remind our players often to ask themselves: How did I make the game (NFL football) better? Did I leave it better than it was left to me?" You can imagine the regret that a player will have if he is not sure that he left his defining effort, his very best, on the fields where he played. You can imagine the injustice he will feel for having cheated himself. No player should ever feel a glimmer of that. Herman will do and say just about anything as a coach to persuade them that the gift owes them nothing, and it will depart at its whim, and that they had better honor it now. When they can. When it counts.

Adjust the qualifications away from the physical ability to perform on a football field, and we're talking about life. To a young parent, the opportunity to make a difference in the life of a child begins the first time that child can be held. The window is thrown wide open in those first years; all the love and the contact and the interaction builds such a healthy foundation for the development of that son or daughter. To delay or postpone that loving and caring is to miss one of the greatest opportunities in life. The "moment" is written large in the outstretched arms of a young child.

That same child will become a student, progressing steadily toward the day when she is independent of the decisions formerly made on her behalf by her parents or caregivers. One of the surest signs of maturity in such a young person is the wisdom to sacrifice personal amusement for the achievement of goals that carry her deeper into a meaningful life—in other words, to study for the test instead of going shopping or trying to beat the video game. These are moments of opportunity for kids to recognize and act upon. They may not always bring the desired result, but if they are approached with discipline and regularity, they become habitual. And the habitual pursuit of opportunities, of making the most of the moment, is a tremendous tool for life experience to carry out of childhood. Herman felt that from the moment he first held his son, Marcus. And while he can't pick him up today like he did then, he holds (hugs) him every time they are together. The responsibility continues.

We must also examine Edwards's belief that "nothing good happens after midnight." The message behind it is to "know when to call it a night." This is a staple piece of advice in the world of sports, where more curfews have been bent and broken in the service of hangovers and dimly remembered conversations than in the building of championships. The hour indicated is adjustable to the moral imperatives of the level of competition—a high school senior's 10 p.m. might correspond to a pro player's midnight—but the message is the same. When we're striving for a goal that is larger and more complicated than a roll of the dice or a moment's entertainment, then willfully placing obstacles in the way of our progress is a losing proposition.

The obstacle may be sacrificing rest and rejuvenation, or it might be associating with people not dedicated to our own best interests. It could be a television watched to the point of numbness, or a computer screen stared at to the threshold of hyperactivity. It may even be the war whoops of our own ids, the idea that whatever makes us feel good has got to be right with the world. Whatever the obstacle, we can see it as an example of bad timing, a stumble, a loss of momentum. We're adaptive creatures, and we may feel—especially when we're young—that we have the savvy and the energy necessary for correcting the course. We see this attitude played out on a daily basis by prominent figures in the fields of entertainment and sports, where talented people vigorously defend their right to be less than they could be, or to simply please themselves at the expense of correct behavior.

But one of our evolutionary rewards as humans is our awareness of both the world within and the world without. We know about rhythm and timing on both an instinctive and an intellectual basis. When we consider the mind-bending variety of rhythms that nature supplies us—rivers flowing, seasons cycling, light, dark, birth, death, and the wind coming "right behind the rain"—and add our own deeper understanding of how to work with and complement these rhythms, then our potential seems boundless.

When we speak of being "in the zone," we're talking about making these worlds mesh. Being "in the zone" describes a state of timing and awareness in which every step, every action, is correct. The football looks like the Goodyear blimp to a wide receiver in this mode. A baseball player armed with this level of concentration waits for a cantaloupe to float over home plate. A guy flipping burgers in this state of mind can serve a drive-through line with a hundred cars in it and not miss a single pickle. A parent or a teacher inhabiting that place finds the words to make the lesson instantly clear, as if she was picking them right off a tree growing next to her. An actor "in the moment" is having a transcendent experience in which imitation and real behavior have become one and the same, with considerable enrichment of the audience. Timing is inherently correct if the preparation has been made and the effort is honest. Because timing will always find its way back to the essential rhythms that guide us in life—if we let them. If we encourage them.

Eliminating the distractions and the interruptions is a necessary first step. You don't want to burn up all your resources before you've had a chance to apply them. No marathon runner wants to show up at the starting line exhausted from a warm up. It doesn't make sense. To get to that enhanced state of mind, the zone, it takes discipline. You can't haul the baggage of bad preparation with you and expect to arrive at that place where you can confidently and instinctively execute. A head coach like Edwards has to remain constantly vigilant, on his guard against those impediments to the plan. "I've noticed in past seasons that when the Jets are playing at home the distractions tend to accumulate," he says. "Tickets, babysitters, the phone ringing with everybody you know at the other end of the line—it can dull the edge that a player needs to have, especially at home where you should have an advantage.

"So I tell the team that whatever they have to do, they have to get it done on their time. If they have to be on the phone, get it done. If there is other outside business to be concerned with, get it done. Get it done when the time is right for that, and come to the field ready to turn an opportunity into a reality. We can't lose our edge, I tell them. We have to be able to win at home, because we don't want to have to go on the road to win playoff games. And to do that you have to establish some kind of credibility at home, so that people don't come into your house and feel like they have a fifty-fifty chance of beating you. Underlying that credibility is the presence of mind that eliminates distractions and recognizes that there is a time for everything that needs to get done."

Execution requires a healthy amount of trust in what you're doing, even when things are not going particularly well. If one was to examine the Jets' fortunes from a strictly outside perspective, there have been times in the past couple of seasons when things looked bleak. The way out of those times is to find the flow once again, the heart of forward progress, where one thing simply follows to another in the right order. So Edwards tells his players, "As long as there were games left, we have to have plenty of hay in the barn. That means we just keep working. And work we do. We would keep coming back and competing and playing hard, and lo and behold, finish a game" (read: won it).

"When each player searches for his own connection to the zone, the result will be the single victory needed. And after that one victory, the team is looking for its renewed sense of connection, and then another one would come. Success building on success, the rhythm coming alive like a good piece of music. It's a beautiful thing when it happens, and it's as strong a reason as you're going to find to explain why people compete. It's not even a matter of competing against another team or individual. Victory, if it comes, is the by-product of us getting to that place where we are performing at our utmost, free and uninhibited. The opposition focuses our energy, but ultimately it's not about beating anybody but rather, about hurrying to the leading edge of one's abilities and letting the correct actions build on one another."

Being on time is a unifying factor. As the Jets players' playbook dictates, it all starts there. Being on time is a simple discipline that can create instant cohesion among groups of players whose styles and customs may be extravagantly diverse. It can do the same for any group with a recognized common purpose, and it works the same on an individual basis. Self-respect doesn't have much of a chance to take hold, if someone is being pushed and shoved by their inability to control that elementary function. But show up on time, and you've done something. You're someone to be reckoned with, when you square up with the first of your obligations. Beyond the individual level, respect blossoms when personal timing and discipline coincides with the needs of the team, the class, or the family. Being on time is the foundation for being in time, when correctness flows unimpeded and the right results become inevitable. That's how the game is played. That's how everything works in this life. You need to be where you're supposed to be. Be on time. No excuses. No explanations.

The Official's Call

"Never missed a kickoff," I often kiddingly brag as I'm arriving to meet someone. And, of course, I haven't. While being on time is vital to Coach Edwards and his team, it certainly is to an official. But it doesn't start on "Game Day" for officials anymore than it starts there for the Jets.

I credit my parents for this. When my mom said, "Dinner at 6:00," I had to be there, at the table, hair combed, hands washed at 6:00. Not 6:01, but 6:00. I guess I really learned this "the hard way." Being late once too often, found myself embarrassed and holding up dinner for my family.

I was always on time to school—actually early, as well as to practices, and games on the teams I played on in high school and college. I can recall when I was in grammar school at St. Therese— well, the nuns would have none of my tardiness and I learned that early on. And for my after-school (playground) activities, I was the first one there. My thinking was that if I was late and they had already chosen sides, I'd be left out. I sure didn't want that.

When I began officiating I was always early to every assignment, forty-plus years and never late. Whenever I experienced a close call of arriving "just in the nick of time" I felt hurried and unprepared. Like the game got away from me. You don't make it to the NFL officiating corps with sloppy personal (timing) habits. Yes, sloppy late is just as much of a habit as punctuality.

For our NFL officiating crew, as referee, I was responsible to see that the crew was ready. Arrive in the city on time (thirty-one years in the NFL, I can't ever recall any official on our crew missing a flight because he got to the airport late. There's that old saying in the airline industry, "If you're not there when they're scheduled to depart, they go without you!"

We have meetings, meals and more meetings the day before (Saturday) the game and on Sunday, mass, then breakfast and more meetings. Everyone must be on time and alert every time. We arrive at the stadium two and half hours before the kickoff. Hurrying to the stadium for a just-in-time (JIT) kickoff is sloppy. You don't last long at that speed.

And, of course, during the game, we "keep the time." That falls to our line judge for game time and to our back judge for the play clock. Although those two clocks are visible to everyone, it is our responsibility to keep them accurate. We constantly remind all our officials—seven in a crew—to always know: the down, the distance (yards to be gained), and the time on every play.

As a referee working along side the offensive huddle, I had to be aware of the huddle time (25/40-second clock). I thought it to be a stupid foul (that's an oxymoron) to be penalized for "delay of game" (too much time expired before the snap of the ball). I would often remind a quarterback when I thought the time was close, by saying, "Be aware of your time" or "Take a look at the clock." I can't recall a time when I penalized a team more than once during a game for "too much time" (delay of game).

One more thing on time. In calling a foul or "throwing the flag," timing is vital. "Don't be too quick; don't anticipate," I reminded myself and each official in our crew, "Let the action happen, read it, and if an infraction occurs, throw the flag—with conviction." The opposite is equally bad—"a late flag," as the announcers may say. And while that "late flag" may be justified, more often it leaves the players, coaches and fans with the thought, "That official wasn't sure." It belies trust in officiating.

Timing is vital to confidence in officiating. We must work at it; we need preparation and study, just as a team does to improve performance.

The legendary Coach Vince Lombardi so instilled being on time to his players, they often called it "Lombardi Time." To them this meant that if Coach Lombardi called a practice or a meeting, say, for 8:00 o'clock, he really meant 7:45.

As Coach Edwards says, "Be on time. No excuses. No explanations."

God may not always come when you want him—but
he's always "on time."   —Unknown

CHAPTER 4

Setting the Chains

There is no right way to do something wrong.

—Unknown

As Roxie Hart, one of the two star characters in the play/movie Chicago says, "Whatever happened to class?" Whatever happened to "please" and "thank you" and "you're welcome"? Where do we learn these important words? At home from our parents, at school from our teachers, at play/work from our friends? Unfortunately, the word "hardly" comes to mind.

Our friends at play or work seem to care little about the kindness that needs to be shown to others. What's wrong with being nice to others? So they can be nice to you in return? It's important to approach kindness and politeness with the attitude that it is just "the right way." Try to approach everything that way—the right way. Let's correct that. Take "try" out of that statement. "Try" is a word that gives us an excuse for failing. So remove "try" from your vocabulary.

Coach Edwards says, "I will" as in "I will do the right thing." In setting your mind for "I will," you strengthen your resolve to accomplish the task. Now, that doesn't mean that you will be successful every time. It does mean, however, that your effort to succeed is focused on the task not on the idea of "trying" to succeed. We all "try" to succeed. No one starts with the attitude that they want to fail. Those are the words of a sure failure.

There's a story about a high school football coach who not only was successful and a great motivator but also cared about his players. He wanted them to be the best they could be.

His team was playing an important first league game of the year against a powerful opponent. The opposition had an outstanding running game and was running play after play around his team's left end. Tommy, the team's starting defensive end was unable to contain the opponent's "sweep" around his end of the scrimmage line. Coach called another player, Billy, off the bench and said; "Now, Billy, watch this play. They are gaining too much ground around Tommy's end. I want you to go in there and stop that play around the end."

Billy said, "I'll try, Coach."

Coach said, "Billy, go sit down, Tommy's trying."

It may be apocryphal, but the message is clear. Billy would "try," but that was not what the coach wanted. Billy's response "I'll do it, Coach" would have shown the confidence that it could be done.

Coach Edwards tells the team, "We are winners." He doesn't even use the phrase "We want to be winners"—as if that idea is off in the future. You must think of yourself, your family, and your team as winners—now! You were born a winner (as the old adage goes "God didn't make no junk"). Therefore, believe that each of us must nurture that nature within. Please understand that no one has won every time or at every thing he or she does. Losses—or setbacks if you will—can only make us stronger if we keep that winning resolve first and foremost in our hearts and minds.

One note about "winning" before we talk about the "secret" of a winning approach. Remember, winning does not necessarily mean you beat the other guy. Winning has to do with making steady progress toward your goal (objective). When you do that you are succeeding (winning). A case in point is the game of golf. You can't win at golf—okay, you can "win" a match or a tournament but you can't beat golf—you can only work at it to get better. There is no "Super Bowl" where you win that game, and the season is over. With golf you just keep playing. It is the challenge of it. So when you keep playing to get better that becomes your goal—your challenge. And why? Sir Edmund Hillary, who scaled—and conquered—Mt. Everest, gives us the answer when he was asked why he would undertake an almost overwhelming task. Sir Hillary said, "Because it is there," meaning that as long as the challenge is there, he will take it. I like that.

Now for the "secret"—the secret to becoming a winner; actually to becoming more of a winner than you are right now. The secret? Always do the right thing! When you make a mistake, stand up to it.

Just be honest—no I didn't say I "try" to be honest, that is an opportunity to have an excuse for failure. (If you didn't pick up on that idea, please go back and reread the idea of eliminating the word "try" from your vocabulary).

Dr. Robert Anthony reminds us, "Trying provides two excuses: an excuse for not doing and an excuse for not having. You can have only two things in life: reasons and results. Reasons don't count."

Now this approach to Edwards's life is not just as head coach of the New York Jets. It extends to all parts of his life. As a son, husband, father, friend to every kid in his football camps—everywhere he goes and to everyone he meets.

Edwards demonstrates by example how "please," "thank you," and "you are welcome" bring people closer together—to be a team as it were. He is the coach he wants to be.

One day on a plane from San Francisco to Atlanta, I met a man who struck up one of those instant conversations. He said hello. I nodded an acknowledgment. Then suddenly he was telling me about some scheme he was working on to cover some losses due to a shift in the dollar-yen values and to finesse bigger expense reimbursements.

I thought to myself, How's the world to survive all the manipulations of people willing to sell their dignity for a dime? No wonder people are burned out and crazy. Dignity is gone. The guy spewed on a little bit and then suddenly stopped. He looked at me and asked, "Whaddya think I should do?" What do I think?

My first thought was, "I don't know this guy. And after just a few minutes of monologue, he's calling for a judgment from a total stranger. Who does he think I am, Dr. Phil?" The guy broke in with a repeat, "Really, what should I do?"

"Tell the truth," I said. "Go to your boss and tell him how your department has become more sensitive to shifts in international currencies, and how it's a joke around the company that the review of expense accounts is sloppy. Tell him you feel crummy about fudging your expense claims and that you'd like to make up for it. Ask him what he thinks that should be."

I was on a roll. "If he fires you, he fires you." I said, "You can find another job, or make one for yourself. Anyone who can work the intricacies of the scheme you described is smart enough to stay gainfully employed if he decides to." I paused, surprised at my directness.

"You asked. So, that's what I think." I was hoping I didn't sound insolent, but it seemed simple to me.

The guy looked a little taken aback. Then brightened up and said, "Huh." He paused a few seconds, and then said, "So you think I ought to go straight in and tell the truth, huh?"

"What would you tell your kids to do?" I asked.

"Huh, yeah," he said. "I see your point."

I unsnapped my seatbelt and took a walk. Maybe my comments had helped the guy, but there seemed little credit to take because it was such an anonymous attachment. Apparently he was searching for advice, probably any kind. I had the feeling that if I had encouraged him to drain his department budget dry, he might have taken to that idea too.

I am discouraged by this example of ethical laxity. It seems so every day. I see it as tied to the general laziness that has crept into our whole society.

By a quirk of mind, the conversation made me recall the feats of courage I witness at the summer games of the Special Olympics. Special Olympians have to give immense concentration to accomplish simple activities, ones that most of us give little thought. It makes you realize how often we give ourselves credit for doing the basics. What's our challenge?

Few of us use anywhere near the percentage of ourselves to achieve great personal triumphs as many Special Olympians use simply to get dressed in the morning. Apparently our generous reserves of skills and energy allow us to squander them on lost days, devising schemes to fudge expense accounts and petty indiscretions. Few of the challenges we face match the unrelenting reality of cerebral palsy, Down's syndrome, and the myriad other conditions and diseases that afflict Special Olympians. We do okay, though, so we congratulate ourselves, forgetting that credit is relative.

What happened to the courage to be strong-minded? Are we waiting to be excited out of our complacency? It's laziness, I think, more than wimpiness. When an emergency arises, we typically come through, glad for the opportunity to shine.

The result of that complacency is that our lives become a string of unplanned events (like my seatmate's "accidental" theft). This kind of stringing is scheming, not pioneering. The alternative is a journey guided by strongly individual choices. One kind of decision-making style creates heroes pumped with good stress, eustress; the other makes liars with distress their due.

The philosophy underlying the suggestion to my seatmate was simple: Honesty is the best policy. The Golden Rule applies, as always. When in doubt, use the easy test of asking yourself if you would be proud of your kids if they did what you were thinking of doing. Please, thank you, you're welcome, and honesty have enduring value.

Back in my seat, I looked at the guy and wondered if he had accepted my advice in the spirit intended. Was he thinking he had done something wrong and should make it right for right's sake? Or was he considering how to go from wrong to right for disguised gain? It struck me that, if old patterns held, he might try to angle some extra advantage from his confession. That might be all right, as long as one wrong corrected didn't lead to another manipulation attempted. Right for right's sake should be simple. Telling the truth should not require planning. It should be easier to tell the truth than it is to tell a lie. Yet, most lies come because at the time it seems easier to slink than stand.

Bad habits, like complacency and me-first schemes, grow out of inattention. You stop noticing them. Then they have you. Habits can be changed. A habit of mindfulness is what does it. It is called self-management. It leads to self-confidence and self-respect.

It's simple, direct, straightforward, but not easy, unless you're out of the habit. In learning theory there is a state of self-assurance called "readiness." It refers to those times when a person is feeling confident enough to act decisively. Decisions are based on knowledge and observation, without resort to emotional add ons such as intimidation and sandbagging. With "readiness," the person is in charge; decisions and actions are resourceful and quick. In these times you are best able to overcome setbacks, act creatively, and make an obstacle merely temporary. You have what is called personal power. You're in your power curve. Emotions are fueling your mind, not obscuring it.

The game of golf again comes to mind: The real test is not keeping out of the rough but getting out once you're in. It's the same in life. Flexibility is desirable. It is also a skill. You can learn it. Life presents us with a constant need to adapt to changing circumstances. Knowing (learning) how to stay "ready" allows flexibility. Flexibility creates time. Time increases choices. To the furthest extent possible, your choices should be up to you. This is what "readiness" is all about.

Arrogance is sometimes confused with readiness. The former is a pale substitute, gorged as it is with too much "self" and false pride. Readiness is cleaner, lighter, not bogged down with emotional vacillation. It's enjoyable, comfortable, nearly self-sustaining, often exhilarating. Arrogance, on the other hand, feeds on itself and even with all its bluster is easily toppled by intimidation. There's no courage in arrogance. Arrogance is about sticking tight and "sticking it" to others.

There's plenty of courage in readiness, though, which is about exploring and moving ahead. When "cooler heads prevail" it's because of their readiness, which you can spot by its chief qualities: a clear-headed quick wit and no emotional baggage. You are in your zone of personal power.

People acting from position power, on the other hand, look quite different, calling attention to themselves and the situation as they do with the noisy folderol of "I'm in charge here!" People in charge of themselves do not have to announce it to others. Yet, you must be in charge of yourself before you can hope to be in charge of any situation.

Thus this motto: The more personal power you take into any situation, the less vulnerable you are to people working from their position power.

Some people fail to exercise their personal power because they stay trapped by negative feelings, most held over from childhood. Parents and teachers usually impose limits as a matter of convenience, some set them negligently, some even maliciously. When a child accepts limits without question, these limits become a fence. He begins to shy away from exploring, himself and his world. The range of his abilities narrows as fast as his imagination. Many adults lost their courage in childhood and haven't looked for it since.

The question is: Can you say you've "grown" or that you are "grown-up" without possessing the readiness to adapt and the courage to explore? Can you act with ease and self-assurance? Can you take a chance? Hold firm? See straight? Set a far-off goal? Set your chains?

Even if you suffered an unfortunate childhood, what about today and tomorrow? Why carry the burden of missed expectations and past setbacks? Memories can be our worst critic, our worst enemy. You are your own best fix-it man, the only one. Living emotionally in the past causes a fixed, unprepared attitude. There's little flexibility and even less clear headedness. Dwelling on a childhood hurt, a cataclysmic romance or job-related disappointment saps your strength and shortens your sights. Your options immediately become fewer. Casting off these negative feelings gives you powerful energy about the present. You'll be more optimistic about the future. When you "come current," you gain the possibility of readiness, of achieving confidence in your instincts, abilities, and goals.

What are your goals? Where could clear-minded self-assurance take you? It is a hallmark of man's evolution that he wants to set goals. He has a restlessness built in. Curiosity drives discovery. If we are settled into ourselves, ready, we will naturally see a place or a promise as a destination. Without the confidence and energy of readiness, nothing much will happen. It is easier to sit tight, not make a move, watch the world go by and try not to care. This is the fool's island of self-imposed limits.

Many of us live by the limits rather than by the possibilities. This is an intriguing aspect of human personality, but it does not need to be the fence we leave around ourselves. The aim is to find the springboard from which you can aspire feeling again and seek whatever goal you yearn for.

Get clear. Be confident. You decide how you set your chains.

The Official's Call

Self-confidence and personal power—not position power as said earlier—are hallmarks of a good NFL official. As I assessed "rookie" officials assigned to our crew, I looked at those characteristics first. Does he possess the self-confidence needed in today's "fish bowl" game? How will he handle a tirade from a Lombardi, Shula, Allen, or Knox? While I have great respect for those I just named, they were given to be fiery and emotional at times. You can't deal with a player or coach's upsetness at a call that goes against his team with arrogance. Fight fire with fire? No way.

In like manner you cannot tolerate (put up with) abuse designed to upset you or take away your focus from your job: game control. We teach NFL game officials what to say and how to say it in order to maintain the dignity of the game.

Honesty—integrity—or doing it the right way is a hallmark of a good official. I have been associated with the NFL since 1960—thirty-one of those years on the field. I am proud to say that never—ever—has an NFL official been involved with a scandal involving honesty. You have heard a player, coach, fan, or team say, "We were robbed, cheated." That's a comment usually designed to cover up something their team should have done to win that game. Never would an official intentionally cheat a player, coach, or team.

Yes, we have made mistakes on the field. We've called a foul that wasn't there (these are called "phantom calls"). We have missed a foul that should have been called (this is called "blowing a call"). I will state unequivocally that these are "honest" mistakes. When an official reviews his performance (it's all on videotape) after the game, he is upset with himself that the "call" was in error. I found, as you have read earlier, just do the right thing. Be honest. And be willing, if necessary, to admit a mistake.

Philadelphia Eagles at Dallas Cowboys 1969. Roger Staubach, Dallas quarterback, rolls left in a scramble play, trips on his own (no defensive contact) and goes down. As he hits the turf, with me, as referee, chasing him, it appears that he is not going to get up and continue to run. In order to protect the quarterback, (my number one priority as a referee) I blew my whistle, thus stopping the play and preventing a defensive player from "piling on." What I didn't see is the ball squirting out of Roger's hands as he went down. When I did see the ball, the Eagles free safety, Bill Bradley, had scooped it up and was racing untouched for a touchdown. Bradley was an all-American quarterback from Texas University and this was his first NFL game back in his home state. Although the Cowboys were considerably ahead, this would be significant in Bradley's first season.

Remember that my whistle "killed the play" and all chances for "Bradley the star" accolades. As I watched Bradley cross the goal line, I also noticed the Eagles coach, Ed Khayat, screaming at me as he was descending from about twelve feet in the air, arms flailing madly. To put it mildly, he was upset. Since I was about 5 yards from him and the Eagles sidelines, I walked over and said, "Ed, 'I kicked it'" (meaning I blew the call). I continued, 'Coach you should have six points on the board, but I can't give it to you. My whistle killed the play." Coach Khayat, always the gentleman, and although visibly upset, said nothing.

Years later, at an NFL alumni event, Coach Khayat said to me, "You remember that Bradley play in Dallas?"

I said, "Sure do, Coach."

He continued, "You remember what you said to me when I was angry with you?"

I said, "Of course, I told you that I 'kicked it.'"

Coach Khayat responded, "When you told me that, you disarmed me. I had no response. The thought went through my head, 'Which one of us hasn't made a mistake."

The chains of honesty are already set. We just need to observe them every day, every time.

You don't have to think about doing the right thing. If you're for the right thing, then you do it without thinking.

—Maya Angelou

CHAPTER 5

Communicating

It was impossible to get a conversation going; everybody was talking too much.

—Yogi Berra

There are yellers, and that works for a couple of years, I think. Maybe.

—Robert Wood Johnson IV

The indiscriminate scattering of all the information available to us in the twenty-first century has created a sonic blunderbuss that threatens the very nature of meaningful communication. Everybody with an axe to grind, a trumpet to blow, or a point to prove seems to be everywhere, all the time, surrounding us with the grating white noise of knee-jerk analysis, opinion, and advice. As Berra, the dependable oracle, points out, it gets to be a bit much. What is communication if not the orderly exchange of information and points of view? These days, it's harder and harder to find, lost in the racket of a society that constantly proclaims its right to speak first, loudest, and longest.

We all recognize this tendency. It's the parent who, disagreeing with a youth league referee's call, ignores the rest of the game in order to rabble-rouse against the official more effectively. It's the assumption that if a phone solicitor calls at dinnertime and manages to exploit our good manners by talking nonstop for two minutes, then the deal is as good as closed. It's the talk radio host who cuts off opposing callers with the sound of exploding TNT, and the audience that guffaws at such disrespect. It's the driver of the rolling subwoofer disguised as an SUV, pulling up to an intersection and annihilating the tranquility of our own cars with the brute force of his sound system. It's the spouse who persists in the belief that every marital disagreement must produce a winner and a loser and that winners know how to use volume more effectively. Give and take? Hardly.

Communication is not a passive exercise. Listening—the quiet art that forms the heart of healthy communication—should approach the aerobic. Not that we have to hear our hearts pounding in our ears, but there should be vigor in our alertness, an undistracted willingness to be there for the other party. The energy with which we absorb the information being sent to us will be equal to the wisdom and fairness of what we ourselves impart. A journalist interested in getting the best possible interview understands this concept. The field of psychotherapy certainly depends on it. And getting the maximum effort out of a team requires a concentrated effort to communicate, to ensure that the message—whatever it may be—is fully received and implemented. In order for this to happen, a coach must not only broadcast his plan, but also lean in close and listen. A good coach (or leader or communicator—the terms are interchangeable in this respect) needs to identify the best route into an individual and tailor the message to run unimpeded on that road.

This is the quality that Herm admired in the coaches he encountered during his youth in and around Seaside and Monterey. He recalls the approaches taken by Jim Cota and Dan Albert, the men who served as his first youth league and high school coaches respectively. Communicating was the best thing they ever did. They would know a guy's strengths and weaknesses; they would know how to talk to that player according to his emotional temperature. Some guys needed a board over their heads, and other guys responded better to a softer touch. That was a key realization for Herm. They were demanding, but they always found the good in the guy and coached around that.

The example of better coaching through heightened awareness of a player's receptivity is one that Herm met again and again as he climbed the football ladder to the NFL. Luke Phillips and Chris Pappas had him for only a single season at Monterey Peninsula College, but their interest in their players was a coaching attribute that Herm observed and respected. What he saw in them is that they accepted players for who and what they were. They had fun with it, and they had a good football team because of it. They coached every guy a little differently, with varying shades of emphasis that amounted to a custom fit for the ideas they were trying to get across. They found the way that was going to work, and Herm became an admirer of their style and sensitivity.

In Philadelphia, Herm met up with Fred Bruney, the defensive backfield coach under Head Coach Dick Vermeil and Defensive Coordinator Marion Campbell. There at the pro level the pattern was strengthened: the best coaching was based on true communication. Information flowed in both directions, and the presumed teacher was himself a student, gathering knowledge and insight about the player he was trying to educate. Bruney was one who was always open to discussion. A player could go and talk about anything with him. He never held his way of doing something above everything else. He never said, "We've got to do it this way, and that's final." He was a great coach, an excellent teacher. He had been a player with Ohio State University and the New England Patriots, so there was a bed of practical experience underlying his guidance. But he was a better tactician. He understood players, and if you made it clear you were going to work hard he trusted you. When Herm went out on the field he never looked over his shoulder. He knew Bruney trusted him.

One of the stronger impressions of Bruney is of his willingness to innovate based on player input. During a practice he once asked Herm, "How are you reading that play so fast?" Herm told him what he was doing, explaining his moves based on his read. This was stuff he'd been doing at MPC and San Diego State. It was almost second nature. And then Bruney said, "Well, how do you know that?" Herm answered, "Because I watch the quarterback before the receiver comes out. He tells me what I need to know." And that clicked with Bruney. They started using that technique on a team basis. There were things they talked about, and Bruney would say, "Hey, we can try that."

A communicative coach will be alert to new ideas that can help his or her program along, and their origin will be of significantly less importance than their usability. The person in true charge of a situation does not hoard information or resist a suggestion because he feels that if he does, his authority might be threatened. Listening and giving fair evaluation is one of the checks and balances that can be applied against the ego. A good idea is a good idea, and successful leaders look for these everywhere—and give credit where it is due.

At some point during the beginning of each season, Coach Edwards gathers the team for a picture that will be used for publicity purposes. The image becomes the public face of the football team, the single portrait of the team as a whole. The picture is a fake. It's not a trick photo. The entire team is actually present, at the same time and in the same place. No cutting and pasting is done to enhance it. There is no digital sorcery performed on it. If what you're led to believe is that the team in the instant that photograph is taken is a unified family of competitors, all equally committed to a common goal—well that's simply not true. Every team in the league perpetrates the same fraud. They take a picture as a team, but the picture is just a picture. It's just a picture until all those people give their hearts to each other. The photo has no authenticity until those men have all earned each other's trust. That takes time, and hard work, and faith, all the way around, from the owner right down to the equipment guys. Once they accomplish that, the picture takes on a new dimension, and it gets lifted out of the realm of the counterfeit.

It also takes a commitment to communicating, and this must begin with the team leaders. Coach Edwards believes he has to start that ball rolling and set the tone and the parameters for the kind of communication that will be sustained. At early points in recent seasons this has meant that he has to be a solitary voice, speaking in clear-cut terms of better days to come when the team has been down and ineffective. That's one thing a coach brings to the table, a *will* that can't be broken or altered by outside factors. The coach's belief has to be immutable, and it has to be broadly disseminated—he can't allow his faith and confidence to be a private affair. A coach must believe in his team, must let them know that they are a good football team that is going to win games, a coach who communicates well keeps telling them that. He has to. It's his job, and he has to make the message consistent.

Is that blowing hot air? Not if he means it. When a team comes around to the coaches' belief—not if but when—it had better not be a mirage. The more you talk about their strengths and about what the team is capable of, and the team observes that the coaches' personality is consistent, and then they have a better chance to reset. They can see that the coach hasn't entered alien territory, and they think, "Hey, if the coach is all right, we must be too." And that's where the passion and enjoyment of a job needs to come in. To truly enjoy the process of taking a guy (or that group of guys) and helping him understand what his strengths and weaknesses are so that he can find the ways to improve his performance is the joy of coaching. No matter how long it takes, "If I believe in my team, that's an absolute value," says Edwards.

You are constantly teaching the veterans as well as the rookies. For that matter, it's true for the coaching staff; there is no point at which anyone involved in the game knows enough to justify thinking that he has achieved ultimate mastery of it. Obviously, the more seasoned the veteran, the easier it will tend to be for him to gather in what you're communicating to him and put it to efficient use. But it's the same process. Every day it's like hammering out that old rock. You keep working away at it, and the chips are flying; you may not see much in the way of a final shape, but you keep going. The chips are the small realizations, the everyday disciplines, and the starting points that will bring the success that is hidden in that rock. And then one day the rock cracks, and the hidden shape is revealed. The man, the player, the team—it all comes alive. It's a blossoming brought by patience and consistency, and it's one of the joys of being a coach.

The commitment to free and creative communication that Herm Edwards found as impressive as he was being coached is something he has strived to make an integral part of his own system. And now it is his turn to impress. Paul Hackett, the Jets' offensive coordinator, is one who has seen firsthand the results of this philosophy. "When he got here, the presence of the man, his forthrightness, his honesty, captured this football team immediately," he observes. "He gets across to the players that he has sat where they're sitting, that he has been through what they're going through. I look at their faces, I watch how they listen, and I see it moving both ways. He has a knack for reaching people. That's what he can do. It happens to be that it's in the world of football, but he can do that. You watch him in practice. One day he'll be out backpedaling, coaching the cornerbacks. The next minute, he'll be over catching a pass in the pat-and-go period. The minute after that he'll be dead serious talking philosophically about your family, the importance of being honest and trustworthy, and being a pro who can be counted on. He'll go wherever he needs to go to deliver that message. The toughest thing in our business is to bring everyone under the same roof, with the same philosophy, pushing and pulling in the same direction. I think Herman has done that, and we're just getting started here. I tell you, it's been fascinating for me."

Elsewhere in the Jets organization this appraisal is shared from a slightly different perspective. Terry Bradway, the general manager, through whom vast amounts of business and personnel information must pass in the day-to-day operation of the team, relishes the simplicity of Edwards's communication skills. "You know, the good thing about Herm is he doesn't even turn his computer on," he says. "He probably knows how, but he doesn't turn it on, and he doesn't really use his cell phone either. Because his attitude is 'If I can walk two doors down the hallway to talk to somebody, I'd rather do that than send him an e-mail.'" Unexpected words, perhaps coming from a key player in a high-tech, information-driven environment, but they underscore the essence of good communicating, which can hold its own in a world full of brain-bursting distractions.

"You can't lose the personal touch," adds Bradway, "because that totally gets it done."

Robert Wood Johnson IV (a.k.a. "Woody") roams the sidelines of Jets' games with an aristocratic calmness befitting the owner of a team that would hire a man like Herm Edwards as its head coach. He is as impressed with Edwards's communication skills as any of his coaches, any of his players, or any of the boys at Edwards's youth football camp. "I spent eight hours with every one of the people we interviewed," he recalls. "We gave them every opportunity to express themselves. And Herm was obviously very impressive during that process. But there's a difference between the interviewing and the doing. He becomes more impressive and more unique the better one gets to know him.

"He never said, 'Don't swear,'" continues Johnson, selecting a parable that is indicative of the Edwards philosophy. "But people around him rarely, if ever, swear, including me or any of the people who might be very accustomed to it, being around a football team. That's an example of how effective he can be with the example he sets. He's not an in-your-face-type guy. But he's a very good communicator. He gets his message across. He's a good salesman. Obviously, he has to be as a coach. You've got to get to the players when they're up, and when they're down. And when they're losing— when they don't get it, or they're frustrated, or they're being beat out—that's when a coach comes in and becomes somebody who can truly make a difference."

In the pantheon of coaches who have truly made a difference, none is more praiseworthy than Don Shula of Baltimore Colts and

Miami Dolphins fame. Johnson holds Shula in particular esteem, and he sees strong similarities between Shula and Edwards. "My favorite coach was always Shula," he says. "I thought Don was very good, because he gave his players a chance to win every year and maintained that for many, many years. And with Herm's style, that's something I think he is able to do. He doesn't have the kind of heavy-handed leadership that people figure out and come to resent, or just say, 'The heck with it.' The yellers, for instance. There are yellers, and that works for a couple of years, I think. Maybe."

The yellers. We all know them. Arteries bulging, eyes bugging out, skywriting with saliva as they make themselves perfectly clear in a voice that endangers nearby windowpanes. We've all been one, at one time or another. How else are we ever going to get the kids out the front door and into the car? What other parenting tool short of corporal punishment will separate two wild-eyed brothers rolling and tumbling through the household, leaving a trail of teeth and fur? How else can we emphasize just how plain and simple the instructions were—which even cattle could have understood—that should have guaranteed success if only they had been followed? As the degree of (what we perceive to be) stupidity, inattention, or indifference seems to rise higher and higher, don't we have a responsibility to register an honest opinion in an appropriate tone of voice?

Meet the wall-of-amps coach. Or boss. Or parent. A little showmanship may be required now and then, because it is very important that we make sure we have their attention. So we make full use of the vocal instrument, and we regard the imparting of our knowledge and experience as a nose-to-nose battle with ignorance and sloth. The people way out on the fringe of the crowd tend to drift away if we don't turn the knobs up to eleven. This may mean that the people in the first few rows get plowed under by our message, but there will always be collateral damage. Some people in fact respond better, or at least without rancor, to this kind of leadership. I refer to the types who need to be whacked over the head with a board, and there are some exemplary players and citizens among them.

The opposite archetype we might refer to as the acoustic coach. Or teacher. Or director. This is a person who subscribes to an economy of style that utilizes the minimum power needed to get the message across. The unamplified support provided by such a leader strives for a one-to-one connection with each person who is in a position to receive the message. If we boil away the team/class/group and condense it to a single receiver, a single pair of eyes and ears, we need to examine which approach is more likely to succeed. If we treat the collective identity as an individual, are we showing it enough respect to keep it open to our message? What strengths or receptive qualities in our subject player/child/student are we appealing to if we yell at them? If we use a quieter approach?

It's a judgment call. Competitive or challenging situations will always call up a degree of emotion, which can be used as an element of preparation. We may choose to amp it up in order to better transmit our own passion in a given situation, in the hope that it will inspire those taking our direction. There are countless successful precedents for this approach. But we have to remember that the louder that wall of amps gets, the more the sound coming out of it is subject to distortion; that's basic rock 'n' roll. We don't want the force of the message to obscure its finer points. We don't want to grind into an emotional sludge the subtleties and the good thinking that went into our ideas. Power for power's sake is discordant and alienating. It's important to know when each style is appropriate, and to err on the side of dignity, both our own and the dignity that belongs to our audience.

My experience has taught me that if you holler at the top of your lungs, the one result you can count on is a headache. I'm inclined to think that beyond a certain decibel level players are not listening anyway. It may look good for TV, and it gives the commentators something to talk about—"Yeah, look at him go, there's the legendary passion"—but it may not have that much to do with winning a football game. Men who are known as players' coaches may be blunt, and wear their emotions on their sleeves, but they also add an undeniably positive and constructive element to it. They are passionate, they tell the truth, and they are loyal. Loyalty to your players won't allow you to compromise their dignity. That's what being a players' coach is all about. It doesn't make you a softy. It makes you understand communicating on a deeper level from both sides of the transaction. Sure, they need a kick in the behind sometimes, but there are ways of going about that. There are ways that Coach Edwards accomplishes that, which preserve the calmness we need to be rational and move things step by step.

If a player messes up, especially with a penalty or some other situation where the correct action or method was painfully obvious, then he has already initiated his own punishment and correction. Edwards has never been a proponent of running up on a guy and jumping in his face. He prefers to walk over and talk to the guy, and not immediately after the play. In those moments, the offending player is least likely to be listening anyway. He may be too busy kicking himself or girding himself for the attack he expects from the coach. You're better off waiting, picking the moment, and speaking to a player in the context of whatever productive relationship has already been established. Edwards finds his teaching voice, goes over what happened, and figures out what needs to be done from there. That's how Coach Edwards works at communicating during the heat of battle, in the hope that meeting halfway will keep the players and the team firmly on the road.

The passion and the dignity can coexist with great synergy, a point made in some fashion by virtually everyone who comments on Edwards's assets as a coach and person. Tom Craft, who played with Edwards at San Diego State and was the head coach there, has long admired the balance of those qualities in his friend. "This is a day and age when everybody's so computer oriented that you tend to lose your people skills," he explains. "Herman's definite: this (football) is a people business. And I think that's why he's gone so far with it. He believes in something and he's really firm about it, real strong about it, and he's pretty relentless on how he wants to get it done. That's an important part of how he leads on the field. But he's a sensitive guy, a very sensitive person who cares about how other people feel. The sensitivity helps the strong will. Together they create real charisma. Those are two valuable assets to have as people skills."

What Herm's old friend and teammate Tom Craft is describing is a state of mind and spirit that resonates through human history. Herm is grateful he possesses some of that and hopes that it remains the framework of his character. Herm takes great pride in his son Marcus and the close communication they have. Marcus has had to endure many times when they couldn't be together. The many years Herm was playing and coaching kept them in different parts of the country. Yet they never lost that ability to communicate. Those times of being apart have brought them closer together.

His love for Marcus is endless. After Marcus achieved so well at

Palma High School in Salinas and Herm had moved onto the Tampa Bay Bucs, he brought Marcus to Tampa to enroll at the University of South Florida. And in 2003, Coach was pleased that Marcus chose San Diego State to play for Tom Craft. Coach Craft provided him with strength and communication that are important to his continuing development. Gentility and strength—when these qualities work side by side—represent our species at its best and most developed. The life of Jesus serves as a fine illustration of this principle, as do the examples set by the prophet Muhammad, Siddartha, and other important religious figures. But we can also picture strapping fathers cradling newborns, or coaches of Little League baseball players giving affable docking instructions at that island paradise known as second base. Football Hall of Famer Rosie Grier comes to mind, his knitting needles clacking away in the grip of sack-sized hands. And there's "Mean" Joe Greene, making his way up the stadium tunnel, sharing that Pepsi for the ages with his young fan. They all take their place alongside the icons, and we can too. Images of the strong bearing forth lightness continue to inspire us, no matter how cynical we may have become.

Forcefulness can always be a tool at one's disposal, but an effective communicator will know when and how energetically to apply it so that, in the final analysis, the message is the thing remembered. Often it will mean communicating on an improvisational basis, trying some of this, trying some of that, adjusting tone and emphasis until we're sure the lines are open and we're being understood. This brings us back to the idea of tailoring the approach to blend with the sensibilities of the person we're trying to instruct or motivate.

Marty Schottenheimer notes with great respect Edwards's ability to adjust his approach. "The quality about him that I admired the most was his great skill at communicating with players and teaching them exactly the way it was to be done," he says. "The lines were always very clear. He's an individual who finds a means for the group to interpret what he's saying. Everybody doesn't understand things spoken in one framework only. Some of us, you can tell us one thing and we understand what you mean, but the same reference point or method of communication to another person doesn't necessarily strike the same chord. And so, what you've got to be able to do is find different ways to say the same thing, so that you can reach the entire group. Herman does that so well."

Further comment on the pairing of passion and creativity is provided by John Lynch, all-pro defensive back who was coached by Edwards during his stint on Tony Dungy's staff. For him, Edwards's most remarkable characteristic is his passion tempered with the determination to be an effective communicator, the even keel slicing through a pool of fire. "When Herm steps in a room, it's hard for the attention not to go to him," Lynch observes, "even though he's not the kind of guy that likes to put the attention on himself. He just has that type of presence that some people have for whatever reason. I think Herm has it because of his passion for the game. He has a respect for the game that's unparalleled. One of the first things he told us is that the shield, the NFL symbol, is not just three initials. It stands for something. He really means that. It underlies everything he does as a coach and a person and drives him. In any setting he's one of those people who has a presence about him.

"He reminds me a lot of Tony [Dungy] in his demeanor," continues Lynch. "There's an incredible amount of fire in him, and he carries that stick in his hand that he'll use when he needs to. But he also used to say you had to be able to forget things in a hurry and put them behind you, to keep that even keel whether you were being successful or struggling." This is the balance point that successful communicators determine for themselves. The dual aspects of effective expression and sensitive awareness, of knowing when to push or use restraint, of the passion and the wisdom, come into play with each other at this point. To embrace them both in the correct measure is to communicate effectively.

"The more time I spent around Herm, the more I learned that he has a gift," Lynch adds. "I think all great leaders know that there are different ways to motivate different people. They don't treat everyone exactly the same. Herm has a great knack for feeling out a person and seeing what makes them tick. Some guys need that pat on the back, and some guys need someone to get in their face. Herm has a great feel for what it is exactly that pushes the buttons with a certain player. There were certain values that everyone was expected to adhere to, but he treated everyone a little bit differently and I think that's one of his great talents, knowing we're not all the same. I don't know if it was the way he was raised, the environment he was brought up in, but he just has that knack for knowing how to get the most out of each and every person or player."

If we follow the root system of any effective leader, we will find a point in their experience where a good example was set and followed. Coach Edwards was fortunate to have had a succession of fine coaches from whom he learned much about football and the relationships that sustain it. But he had a clear start in all matters of life and communication before he ever donned a helmet and hip pads. From his parents he received the gift of a truth that has provided a strong foundation for all of his adventures as a person, player, or coach. He learned very early from them that you judge people by their character. It's not how much money they make. It's not the color of their skin. It's not where they live, nor is it about how they look. Sit and talk to people. Find out what they are, and you'd be surprised how much you have in common.

Sit and talk to people. Study their maps. Their weather. Their terrain. Listen with enthusiasm to the stories and concerns that make them unique. Learn the best route in, and don't hesitate to make the trip. Find out what they are, and you'd be surprised how much you have in common. Despite the odds and the obvious difficulties, there will always be a basis for some kind of mutual interest. At the very least, there is shared humanity. If we honor it within ourselves, we need to do likewise for the people we come into contact with.

Former Eagles coach and mentor Dick Vermeil is one who dedicated himself to the art and business of communicating well. He's very competitive and very disciplined, yet would never come across as bendable; he manages to build trust levels with his players that would have those guys running through walls for him. Some people say he's hard, but players don't run through walls for men who only wield authority. They run through walls for men whom they respect and who respect them. They run through walls for men who have taken the time and trouble to find out more about them, and communicate honestly and directly. Players will be loyal to a coach like that, but it will be the man first and the coach second. They'll respond to the character of the man, and football, however important, will be of secondary concern. Players will go the extra mile for a coach—an individual—they trust and who has unshakable trust in them. When the communication works that well, players have been given part ownership of the team and have been made partners in its fate. There is little more that a player could ask for.

Coach Edwards reminds us, "I work on that every day."

As an observer of the style employed by Coach Edwards when addressing his team before, during, and after numerous games, I can attest that he gets his message across. He ensures that his ideas, comments, and directions are both fully delivered and fully received. His energetic and imaginative dedication to true communication is one of his hallmarks as a leader.

In team meetings populated by players, coaches, and others vital to the club's game performances, Coach Edwards never fails to make eye contact with each person present. No one nods off, zones out, or carries on a side conversation when he has the floor. When he speaks he commands the floor, from front to back and side to side. He commands the floor in much the same way that a performer like Sinatra, Bennett, or Streisand will compel attention on stage. He does it with personal power, not position power. There is a tremendous difference between the two.

Position power declares, "I am the head coach, so you'd better listen to me." Personal power wins people over by informing them "I have an important message that you need to buy into in order for our team to win." There are no threats or heavy-handed intimidation tactics. He comes to his team plainly, simply, and most important, honestly. He tells them the truth. "This is what we must do to win." Notice the word "we," not "I" or "you people—you guys—you players." Coach Edwards talks with the players, not at them.

He carries that philosophy to the coaches. He has one-on-one discussions on a daily basis with his offensive and defensive coordinators. Uniting in pursuit of a win, they establish and fine-tune a game plan. It isn't dictated by the head coach; it is coauthored by the staff. This communication holds true for the other position coaches and the rest of the dedicated crew. Important in these exchanges is Herm Edwards's ability to listen. His mind is always open to new ideas and fresh thoughts as to how the Jets can do it better. When I say always open, I need no qualifier; it is just that. Always open. Now, that doesn't mean that there is always agreement. However, when disagreements occur, Coach Edwards is diligent at maintaining open lines of discussion so that a satisfactory result can be realized. He is firm but fair when making a final decision, as every leader must lest he relinquish his responsibility and the trust that comes with it.

The Official's Call

As I watched that process take place day in and day out, I could not help but reflect on the opportunity presented to me as an NFL game official. Twenty-five of my thirty-one years in the game were spent as a referee—the crew chief, or the head coach as it were. The one on one, the constant eye contact, and the open mindedness so characteristic of Coach Edwards reminded me of the communication so necessary in officiating an NFL game.

Each crew consists of seven positions: a referee, an umpire, a head linesman, a line judge, a field judge, a side judge, and a back judge. Each individual is responsible for his own physical training and conditioning in order to prepare himself for an elite performance every Sunday. As the crew chief, I monitored the effort of every man in our crew to ensure that we were ready to call the kind of game required of us by the league representing the finest football players in the world. This I could achieve primarily as an observer. But if, in my estimation, one of the members of our crew had fallen short in his preparation, and was not ready to deliver the top physical effort that was always required, then it was my responsibility to inquire and insist on changes and improvements.

The expression "A chain is only as strong as its weakest link" is axiomatic throughout the range of human group experience, and especially so in relation to team sports. This is as true for the Jets as it is for an NFL officiating crew. Communication is more than the meaning held in words. It is the relationship between two entities that have some basis for interdependency. It is the information carried back and forth across the gap, sometimes directly, sometimes more subtly, but continuously. It rests on observation of all aspects of your team. Or your family—parents must ensure that each child is doing what he or she is supposed to do to learn and grow into a responsible adult. Observing and communicating with your children about proper eating habits, study habits, personal ethics, adequate sleep, and all the other governable aspects of their behavior are no different than what Coach Edwards does with the Jets or what I did as a referee.

The example set by a coach who maintains a regimen of his own is not new. Such legendary coaching figures as Vince Lombardi, Tom Landry, George Allen, Don Shula, Bill Walsh, Dick Vermeil, Marty

Schottenheimer, and yes, even John Madden, all had their own phys-ical workouts, and they maintained an element of solidarity with their players in that kind of practice that nothing else could simulate. As a referee, I, too, felt that same responsibility to communicate lead-ership and partnership. I always believed that an official sharing the field with athletes should look like one. Running side by side with the best players in the sport requires training. An overweight, huffing official who can't move to the best position for making a call is a dis-grace to his profession and to the sport itself. My philosophy remains one of working out only on those days that end in "y" (meeting rea-sonable goals for cardiovascular conditioning and weight training). During my NFL game Sundays, of course, the three hours of con-stant, concentrated movement would suffice for that day's exercise.

Another aspect of Coach Edwards's orientation to communica-tion is his emphasis on mental preparation. Again, he does this by example, by continuously preparing himself. Knowledge of the chal-lenges posed by each week's upcoming game and the team's plan for it are vital to him. He knows it cold, and well he should, because the next task is equally vital. He must communicate every detail of the plan to every player on the team, knowing that according to the "weakest link" axiom, the team will be successful only to the degree that its least familiar member is able to understand and execute it. Coach Edwards uses team meetings to deliver the broader strokes, and then shifts to one-on-one conversations with coaches and posi-tion players. Information is not left in undigested lumps in the club-house. It gets broken down first by the head coach and then by his assistant staff and by the players themselves, doubling back and restating until the intent of the plan and its implementation are clear.

My definition of communication is this: "Communication is the response you get." Coach Edwards bases the effectiveness of his communication on how his team performs on any given Sunday. While winning is the ultimate criterion, he will be satisfied if the team executes in concert with what he has communicated about the game plan.

When a team's preparation is tested against another team's, it may be found that the opponent had the better players where they needed them, or simply that the other team executed its own game plan better on that day. Thus, losing does not signify that your communication was faulty or insufficient; it signifies that your team's execution was not up to the level of your opponent's in head-to-head competition that day.

The same level of preparation is necessary for an NFL officiating crew. All seven members of the crew must take personal responsibility for their mental readiness to participate in the game. Their knowledge of the rules must be quick and flawless, their understanding of the philosophy behind interpretation of the rules must be complete and unwavering, and their mechanics (i.e., physical positioning during each play) must be beyond dispute. Then it becomes the responsibility of the referee to mesh the contributions of the other six men in his crew. He can leave no pre-game detail unattended, and he must make sure that all necessary specific information has been adequately transmitted to his crew.

In the world of professional football, communication takes yet another step when a team is debriefed after a game. This is a follow-up session in the clubhouse during which the head coach talks with his players and coaches. He compliments them on what they did well and points out areas that need improvement. As handled by Coach Edwards, it is not a pronouncement or a judgment passed on that day's effort—there is no finality to it. It is guidance in an ongoing effort to achieve the team's potential. On Monday he and his coaching staff get down to cases, discussing in detail the good, the bad, the ugly and what needs to be done before the team's next outing. Then the cycle is reset as the plan filters down to the individual team members again, and they contribute their own ideas and concerns.

The post game evaluation is as important for an official as it is for a player, coach or team. As the Referee, I created a self-evaluation form for each member of our crew to fill out after every game. Self-evaluation meant just that: the purpose was for each official to review his performance in that game. The evaluation form reminded him to grade his preparation, rules knowledge, mechanics (positioning on each play) and crew coordination on the game just concluded.

In addition, of course, was the videotape of each game including instant replay reviews. Every official in every game is graded (evaluated) on every play, every call (fouls are called "calls"), every no-call (those fouls that should have been made) by the NFL Supervisor of Officials. That grade is entered into a database and tabulated at the end of each season. Officials are assigned to post season (playoff) games on the basis of their game performance (evaluations). Only the top graded officials are assigned to playoff games. Every official works diligently to achieve playoff status. Top performance in every game is the goal of each official.

Open communication is an ongoing process in the officiating ranks as it is with every NFL team.

Herman, Sr.—Master Sergeant US Army, Died 1978

Martha Gertsner Edwards—Born in Germany
Moved to USA as Mrs. Herman Edwards

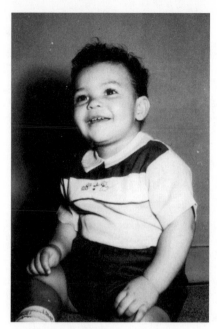

Herman as a young boy—nickname "Bobie"
(German for pretty boy)

Herman and sister Irvina

Herman backyard where "The Broom" was created

Herman with a couple of his MPC Coaches

PHILADELPHIA EAGLES

HERMAN EDWARDS   S   Compliments of Frito-Lay, Inc.

Herman #46 Cornerback with Philadelphia Eagles

Herman's love and respect for his "Mom and Dad" was never ending

Herman #46 during San Francisco game

Herman begins his coaching career in the
Kansas City Chiefs Minority Fellowship Program

Herman as Tampa Bay Buccaneer Defensive Backfield
Coach in old sombrero (Bucks former Stadium) with a fan

Lia and Herman with son Marcus as a
Wide Receiver for the University of South Florida

Lia and Marcus

Lia and Herman at home

Herman explains TYF Football Camp rules to kids

Herman always has a smile around his TYF Football Camp

January 18, 2001—Herman named Head Coach of
New York Jets (L-R) Terry Bradway, General Manager,
Herman, Lia and Robert (Woody) Johnson, Jets Owner

Coach Edwards and Author Jim Tunney

Coach Herm Edwards with Kansas City Chiefs President Carl Peterson

"Mom" Martha as she was at the first printing of this book

CHAPTER 6

Striving and Thriving

Everyone agrees courage is a virtue, but just what is "courage"? Are we born with a certain amount of it and that's all there is to be? Or can we develop it, like our biceps? A central attribute of courage is the ability to perform well in spite of tension or fear, to be able to execute as skillfully and deliberately in tight spots as in ordinary circumstances. Many tend to idealize physical courage. We make instant heroes of people who go to war, confront a mugger, or put their bodies in harms' way. That kind of fear is palpable, visible, easily appreciated.

More often though, the challenges we face today are emotional or intellectual, not physical. Career shifts, office politics, international terrorism, rebellious teenagers, errant spouses, factory closings, dented fenders—these are our more common threats. We face them every day, never earning hero status for surviving them. Even so, the goal is to wade through the muddles and wrangle down the hassles without losing the energy to dream. Our purpose is to "huddle up" and achieve a goal. What fosters the self-reliance to stay in there, tackling issues as necessary and spurting forward every chance possible? What mental glue binds hardiness with patience to make tenacity? What separates the doers from the hopers? What is the everyday courage of emotional and intellectual hardiness? Sometimes you see a situation better from the reverse angle. Let's look at what courage is not.

Courageous actions are never rash, ruthless, sneaky, impetuous, blind, or unimportant. Neither is courage pushed out of you by pressure from others. You're acting from your own decision, not on orders from bosses, coaches, sergeants or peers. Courage is a private experience, self-made.

When all the right qualities are working together, you get the attribute Vince Lombardi, legendary coach of the Green Bay Packers, called mental toughness. Lombardi said his winning teams were built on four principles: self-discipline, self-sacrifice, mental toughness, and teamwork. Coach recognized that without all four, he couldn't reasonably count on his players to focus hard enough and long enough to out-execute the opponent in any circumstance, and that's what makes a winner. "I'll give you my playbook," he would say, "and the Packers will still win, because we'll execute better than you." That wasn't arrogance talking, just a belief in those four principles.

Lombardi believed in his formula and tolerated no slack from his players. He coached hard to get what he wanted, and he expected his players to want it as badly as he did. He knew that each player had to first win the head fight: each person has to be, individually, a victor over his own uncertainties, confusions, doubts, and distractions before he could be valuable in making the team victorious. Conviction, too, is a private experience, self-made.

Coach Edwards believes there's a difference between the kind of focus and self-control that Lombardi talked about and plain old "hard work." It has become popular to consider anyone who "works hard" a "workaholic," and therefore a candidate for an early heart attack, stress-related diseases, etc. This is mistaken. Hard work isn't stressful: working hard without seeing positive results is. Stress doesn't kill you. *Distress* may. In the same vein, there's a difference between tenacity and mental toughness. Yes, you need to have determination, to keep trying, to never give up, but *mental toughness means you also have the self-control and focus to limit your efforts to only the ones that are effective.*

It's like the guy who wants to get out of debt so he decides to trade his Porsche for a BMW instead of accepting his uncle's offer to inherit the family Chevy. He may cry about making "hard choices," but he didn't make the one that would get fast results. Edwards believes, as would Lombardi, that he didn't have the "toughness to commit."

Take tennis, as another example. Anyone who wants to improve at tennis has the same goal: not to lose more than one point in a row. If you never lose two points in a row, you will never lose a game or a match. But to play that tight, to control yourself carefully enough not to have a "bad streak," you have to work on the narrowest goal that will assure success. And that narrowest goal? Focus on only one point at a time. This ability is what mental toughness is all about—the power to focus forcefully and "do it right the first time, every time."

When the competition matters, whether it's the Jets against the Dolphins, or unpaid bills against dollars in the bank, the "winners" will be those who make the strong choices of conviction and commitment. Some people have a greater natural ability to honestly evaluate cause and effect. When asked to call the shot, they assume, with self-assurance and a sense of dispatch, that they can do something about the problem. They don't assume the problem is intrinsic and become fatalistic. It's the difference between a *doer* and a *hoper* or maybe even a "tryer."

To test yourself, check how attached you are to a goal you desire. "Workaholics" and "hopers" see their goals as something outside themselves. They may not express it that way, but that's the way they sense it. Doers, the ones who have learned "mental toughness," feel the goal is coming straight out of their guts. They feel connected to the effort and responsible for getting themselves from where they are now to where they want to be. They're not waiting for "the chance of a lifetime." They're making chances for themselves—chances to succeed.

> Play fast, play hard, play smart!
> —from New York Jets Playbook

It takes a lot of courage to "step up" and play; it needs preparation and self-sacrifice to make a player (read: person) reach peak performance.

Why do athletes always want to do their best? The answer is obvious. First, it's their job. "Their job?" Well, we all have "jobs." Jake, the high school senior, has a "job." His parents have a "job"; doctors, lawyers, teachers—the list goes on—have "jobs."

Yet, we can't always see others doing their "jobs" or if we do, we

may notice that they are not consistently striving for peak performance. Unfortunately, when someone does their "job" unethically, we
see their wrong doings. The Enron, WorldCom, Imclone, Health
South type of CEOs and "leaders" become very visible. Wouldn't it
be a pleasure to know about all the "good things" leaders do for others?
To know on regular, daily, almost play-by-play basis how each han-
dles success and failure as well as a given game plan. We surely
could learn from that. Coach Edwards says, "When a player on our
team stops that effort or slacks off, he is cut or traded or dropped
from the team and thus loses his job. He has no tenure or job security
protected by some social laws. He is just simply—gone!"

What if we required that same professional approach to each of
us in our daily lives? Would there be more pressure? How could we
insure our "job" security? Edwards learned that early on. Thus he
developed the philosophy of "play fast, play hard, play smart."

Play fast! We can see that in a football T*E*A*M (Together
Everyone Accomplishes More). They run onto the field! They run
from their sideline benches to their huddle on the field. They run
from the huddle to their positions. Why not walk?

Running creates energy. Running creates enthusiasm. Running
creates spirit.

Now that's not to suggest that you run to your job. While that
may make you "look foolish," you will find that it does create energy
that inspires you. So if *running* to or at your job is not in your social
mode, what can you do to create enthusiasm for your job? Athletes
use the word "hustle." Coach Edwards expects his players, his coaches
and yes, even the NFL game officials to "hustle." Edwards himself
hustles. Parents, teachers, business folks hustle—to their jobs and at
their jobs and from their jobs. Hustling does create enthusiasm—a
sense of urgency to get your job done.

Incidentally, there is nothing in any job description that says it is
your employer's or your teammate's responsibility to create that
enthusiasm for you. Your enthusiasm must come from you. No one
can assume that responsibility except you!

Your enthusiasm comes from you! No one else! Enthusiasm for
your life, your job, your family is created and maintained by you. Simply
put: it is your A*T*T*I*T*U*D*E! Positive or negative, it is you. The
old saying: is the glass half-full or half empty? You provide the substance
of that glass. You make it half-full or spilling over the brim.

A positive mental attitude (PMA) is essential in everything you do. Whether it is fixing something around your house, mowing the lawn, "sweeping up" the leaves in your yard ("Don't be afraid of the broom!"), or whether your job is as a student, parent, teacher, coach, lawyer, doctor, etc. you are responsible to bring a positive attitude to that job.

Although an advocate of "positive" attitude, one can also bring a negative, or maybe even worse, an apathetic attitude to what you do. Wow! How many people around you just don't seem to care about their jobs? Too many. One could assume with some certainty that if they are apathetic toward their job, they probably carry that same attitude about themselves. They probably just drift along with no purpose to their lives. Like the proverbial "ship without a rudder"—it just drifts along.

One more thing about positive versus negative attitude: if you discover (hopefully you will discover) that others who work around you or in your community or in your church, or wherever, avoid including you in their discussions and their activities, perhaps you need to look at your attitude. Is it negative? I am certain you would agree you don't want to work with negative people. Some advice about "negative people"? They pull you down. It's funny (read: strange) how others' negative attitudes can and will affect your attitude. Avoid these people. Don't walk away from negative people—run!

Coach Edwards and his staff take great care to research a player's background before drafting him or trading for him. He knows from experience how much a "bad apple" (read: poor behavior/poor attitude) can be negative influence on the team. It works that way in any group e.g., family, club, team, business, etc.

So how do you keep your attitude positive? Create or gain that positive attitude through observing others who do their job with joy and enthusiasm. Reading books including the Bible or similar epistles help create positive thoughts. If you think it won't work, it won't. If you think it will work, then your actions give that thought a chance.

Take the huddle as an example. The quarterback calls a play and then commands, "Break!" which means, "Let's do it!" "Let's get this play right." If the guard or any other player leaves the huddle to go to his position and says to himself, "It will never work!" "It won't!" The "play" must be executed by every member of the T*E*A*M with the same positive attitude in which it was designed. Remember, in football, every play—repeat— *every play* is designed to score a touchdown.

Thus, every player must "buy into" that play. He must accept his role, reminding himself as he gets ready that "If it's to be, it's up to me!" No one on a team—all eleven in football—is exempt from that attitude.

Some will say: "There it is, talking attitude again," but why not? Truth is, we begin and end our actions from how we perceive our jobs to be. Whether our attitudes become hardened remnants of a bad experience, which thicken the blanket of self-protection, or whether our perceptions remain resilient and expansive with prospect, it's up to us.

We all suffer setbacks. More frequently, we suffer from our own foolish behavior or lack of effort that a job or project or a play in a game deserves. The difference is in how much vigor we give to our lives. How we react to events and their consequences has to do with what we want from and for ourselves. What do you want?

Play hard! Edwards's second focus is on "playing hard." That means giving your best—every ounce of what you have to give— every time. Slacking off or not feeling that your best effort is required is not an honest approach. Some may look at this "play hard" effort as too stressful.

Stress is getting a lot of bad press these days. Plenty of money is being made on books and tools to relieve it. Spas are sprouting up everywhere to provide a place to refresh muscles and mind. New ways of temporarily relieving stress are everywhere and always have been. It's no wonder people seek convenience. They want to believe that reading a book or having a massage will create a less stressful life. These attempts overlook the core problem—stress is natural. All living contains or inspires stress. No amount of convenience or stress-relieving vacations will make it disappear, nor should we aim for that. The trick is to make a distinction between bad stress (distress) and good stress (eustress). Consider that we all have stressful decisions to make. Too many stressful decisions make a stressful day. Too many stressful days make a stressful life. Too many stressful lives make a stressed out community, whether corporate or residential. Taken together, you get a picture of one choice for modern living, a poor choice. There are distinctions to be made.

Picture the Jets quarterback, Chad Pennington, approaching the line, placing his hands under the center's rear end, looking across at defensive linemen, 6'5", 300 pounds or bigger, linebackers, 6'7", 285 pounds who can run as fast as running backs, all of whom are about to attack him (the quarterback), knock him to the ground—every play. Seventy to eighty times in an NFL game. How does a quarterback look at stress? He loves it! He wouldn't want to be any place else on Sunday afternoon. He knows that if he "plays hard" he will conquer any fear or any stress that he may have. Stress is ubiquitous. It surrounds us as much as gravity does, and like gravity, it has dynamic tension. It holds things together and helps us.

Edwards tells of a play that happened his second year with the Philadelphia Eagles. They were at the Meadowlands—now the Jets as well as the New York Giants home field—playing the Giants. Fourth quarter. Giants 17, Eagles 12. Thirty-one seconds left. All the Giants had to do is run one play—or even a "kneel down" by the quarterback and the game would be over. Joe Pisarcik, Giants quarterback, didn't like the idea of a "kneel down" so, at the snap of the ball he attempted to hand it off to fullback Larry Czonka. The Giants were on about their thirty-yard line. All Czonka had to do was take the ball, get tackled or just fall down. Defensive teams in that situation often just "go through the motions" to get the game over with.

Herm never believed that as a player—at Monterey High, MPC or San Diego State—and doesn't today. "You play hard—every play," he tells his players. And so he did. As a cornerback, he lined up on the line of scrimmage on that play and charged into the backfield. The ball was fumbled—Pisarcik said Czonka didn't take the handoff; Czonka said Pisarcik fumbled the exchange—who cares, it was a fumble in the Giants backfield. The ball took one bounce—right into Herm's hands and he sprinted twenty-six yards into the end zone. Eagles touchdown. Eagles won 19-17.

"Miracle of the Meadowlands."

Why did that happen? The message, as Yogi says, is loud and clear. "It ain't over 'till it's over." Never quit. Play hard—every time.

The Jets now play in the Meadowlands and there are 80,062 seats in that stadium. Yet, everywhere Edwards goes it seems like two hundred thousand people or more said they were there that day. ESPN and NFL highlights have been showing it for over twenty-five years—the "miracle" never ends.

Both teams—the Eagles as well as the Giants—now laugh about the "miracle." In fact, the next year, 1979, Joe Pisarcik was traded—of all places—to the Eagles. Bill Bergey, an all-pro linebacker on the Eagles team, was a great kidder. Herm's locker was right across from Bergey's, who kept a football in his locker. Every time Pisarcik would come into the locker room, Bergey would take the ball, roll it onto the floor of the locker room, and say, "Okay, Herm, show us just one more time." All the guys would break out laughing. It was a great healer and reinforced the bond the team had but also reminded them to "play hard—every time."

Playing in the Super Bowl (as the Eagles team did in the 1980 season), going in to ask for a raise, speaking before your peers, any challenge that you see as positive, can be an energizing one. If you strengthen your self-confidence by talking your way through the challenge, by mentally preparing, by being ready, the dynamic tension of striving will not be nearly as fearful. Your clear-headedness and readiness will develop a sense of mission.

Fears grow from the seed of self-doubt. What causes that? Why do we doubt our ability to survive the day with distinction when all of us, after all, got through childhood, and childhood is a whole lot more surprising, uncertain and unfathomable than our regular, more regulated lives as adults? What did we miss in that education called growing up that made us lose our confidence? Why does it get more difficult to stay involved with discovery and self-discovery? Do we really want life to settle down, get ordinary, surpriseless and even? Why would we want a flat life, except out of laziness or fear? Why should we expect something to happen which, by the very nature of life, never will? Stress won't go away, but our ability to make wise choices for ourselves will create an energy for achievement.

Play smart!

That means prepare, be ready, keep your poise. Let's look at another example of preparation. Jerry Kramer, the right guard of the magnificent Green Bay Packers line during the decade of the 1960s tells a story from one of his early years under Coach Vince Lombardi. Kramer got "chewed out" one afternoon for missing a block in practice. It bothered Kramer so much that he couldn't do anything right the rest of that afternoon practice session. This upset Lombardi who told him, "If that's the way you're going to practice, turn in your uniform. You don't belong on the Green Bay Packers."

Kramer left the field and planned to turn in his uniform. He was sitting disconsolate in the locker room when Lombardi came in and took him aside, "Somehow I want you to understand," Lombardi said, "you're going to be one of the greatest lineman in the NFL. That is if you practice every block, every move as if it counts, as if every play means that game. Get yourself ready. Practice starts at 8:00 a.m. tomorrow."

Remember: practice doesn't make perfect. Only perfect practice makes perfect.

Incidentally, during the "Ice Bowl," December 31, 1967, the NFL championship game between the Green Bay Packers and Dallas Cowboys at Lambeau Field in Green Bay, Kramer made the block that allowed quarterback Bart Starr to "quarterback sneak" two feet across the goal line to beat the Cowboys with no time remaining. The temperature was thirty-one degrees below zero at the time of that block. Was Kramer ready? Had he prepared himself for that block? The answer is, obviously.

Coach Edwards has a strong urge to be prepared in coaching the Jets. As it was for Coach Lombardi, Edwards has always seen the value in taking time to prepare—in high school, in college, with the Eagles and now more than ever as head coach. As Ron Johnson said, "I thought when I saw Herm running, 10-12 hundreds, that was all he did to work out. Then I realized he had worked out much longer before me and those hundreds were just his 'cool down.'"

Head Coach Edwards's daily schedule is one of enthusiasm, reminding himself how important that is. His "enthusiastic day" starts at 4:00 a.m., up and off to the Jets training complex. He works out: running, weight training, and the like. It prepares him for a day of meetings with players, coaches, administrative staff, the press, and everything else that may come along. He just doesn't feel that he will give the right impression to all those around him unless he is physically and mentally prepared to give his best effort *every time, every day*.

And, of course, that daily mental preparation also comes from reading passages from the Bible. That book and those readings are as much a daily part of Edwards as brushing his teeth. Mental preparation is based on a belief in God. Herm thanks Him every day for the privilege he has given to Him as a son, husband, father and head coach. Those daily mental exercises prepared him to do his job better.

As you have read earlier about Lombardi, preparation—both physical and mental—is the key. And, yes, of course Edwards does "get after" the players—and coaches—sometimes, as Lombardi did. All too often, a player at this level starts reading his press clippings that he is "the best" at what he does. It's important that Edwards reminds the players of his basic principle: *"It's the will, not the skill."* All players at this level have superior skills, but it's their "will" to prepare, to make themselves better and to make the team better and, ultimately, to play in and win the Super Bowl Game—the Jets goal every year.

How much better can a player, a coach or a head coach be? No one knows. But Edwards does know that he must always find out how much there is to learn. Oliver Wendell Holmes reminds us, "Most of us die with our music still in us." Herman states, "I want to use *all* my music."

Another aspect of playing smart is: keep your poise. As you may have read earlier, Edwards fortunately had some great mentors: his dad and mom, Coaches Cota, Albert, Phillips, Pappas, White, Gilbert, Vermeil, Peterson, Schottenheimer, and, of course, Dungy. Coach Tony Dungy and he have many similar characteristics. Dungy was a great teacher. Although Herman's style is a little fierier, perhaps more than Dungy's, he learned, especially in times of stress, that he needs to keep his mind clear.

"If you can keep your head, when others all about you are losing theirs," said Rudyard Kipling in his poem "If." (That poem in its entirety is included in this book because every word, every paragraph has meaning about keeping your poise.) The lesson Edwards seeks, as head coach is that maintaining his poise is vital to the direction of the team. That's what is meant by "playing smart." Emotional, high energy, of course, are musts. However, you can better perform at your peak if you have your "wits" about you. A boxer needs to avoid "getting mad" at his opponent. A boxer's collected coolness under pressure will allow his mind to control his boxing techniques, i.e., the way he has practiced and thus execute properly.

The old saying, "It's okay to have butterflies (nervousness) in your stomach. However, it's important that you get those butterflies to fly in formation." Self-control. Poise.

The Official's Call

It was said of Robert Louis Stevenson that he "wanted only to be great, a simple wish that precludes distraction." That's the straight-on ambition and mental toughness as I understand it. As I strove to achieve as an NFL referee, I wanted to be the best. No, I'm not trying to outdo others; I'm just doing what I could to be the best I could be. It took more courage than I thought it would. It took more courage than I thought I had. Self-doubt has a way of creeping into your thinking even when you want to keep it out. You can keep it out. It's called "keep on keeping on!"

As an NFL official, for thirty-one years, working twenty-nine post-season assignments, which included three Super Bowls, and ten championship games as well as some of the most famous games in NFL history, I had to always keep my poise. To deal with an outburst of anger from a coach or a player or seventy-six thousand fans in the stadium, yet not to let that outburst affect my judgment was my task every Sunday—or on Monday-night football (twenty-five of them!). Poise, self-control, and focus on your task as an official often determine whether or not you can keep the game under control. Remember: you need to control yourself before you can maintain control over any situation.

It was a Monday night in Soldier Field, Chicago, Illinois. Yes, it was that Monday Night—"MNF! Are ya ready for some football?" The New York Giants were in to play the hometown Chicago Bears, September 14, 1987. A historic game! Historic because not only was it the first MNF of that season, the kickoff for ABC on national television; it was the first time back-to-back Super Bowl champions played in the first MNF game of the season.

The Giants had defeated the Denver Broncos in Super Bowl XXI in the Rose Bowl, Pasadena, California, 39-20 on January 25, 1987. The Bears had defeated the New England Patriots 46-10 in Super Bowl XX in New Orleans on January 24, 1986. Now they were paired—the two best of the last two seasons. It was not a preseason ("exhibition" as some call it) game. This counted toward a winning record for the 1987 season. Historic!

Third quarter. Score: Bears 24, Giants 7. Giants' ball. Third down and two on their own twenty-eight-yard line. Quarterback Phil Simms barks out the play at the line of scrimmage. Ball is snapped.

Simms drops back to pass. The "rush" from the Bears defense was fierce. Just as Simms starts to throw, Bears defensive end Wilbur Marshall is on top of him. The ball flies out of Simms's hand and bounces on the ground. I instantly blow my whistle and signal (arms waving across my body) "incomplete forward pass." Steve McMichaels, the Bears defensive tackle, picks up the ball and runs into the end zone. Touchdown Bears!

But wait. I have declared (by my whistle and actions) that it was a forward pass when the ball hit the ground, thus, it should have been an incomplete forward pass. Play over. Bears' fans, 67,704 of them, boo loudly and disagree. Up in the booth (press box) we have an instant replay official (IRO). This was the second year of the instant replay (to either verify or overturn the on-field official's call). More on the instant replay system later. Now at this "historic MNF game," we didn't have just any IRO; we had Art McNally, supervisor of officials, who had flown that day from the NFL headquarters in New York to Chicago to be on the job as IRO. McNally reviewed that play and tried to communicate to our umpire on the field, who had a walkie-talkie, what he (McNally) was seeing on the instant replay monitor.

The communication system failed. Remember the NFL was only in its second season of using this system. I was then informed that McNally wanted to talk with me on the phone located behind the Bears team bench. I ran over to that area—remember, I just took away (by my declaring this was a forward pass) a Bears touchdown. At that moment I was not the Bears' most favorite official.

I picked up the phone and said to McNally, "I'll have a cheeseburger, diet coke, and hold the fries." There were 67,704 people in Soldier Field, about seventy million watching on television and I am ordering lunch.

McNally said, "What?"

I said, "Never mind, what have you got up there?"

He said, "We are ruling that play a fumble." If a fumble it was to be, the Bears would have a touchdown.

At that point, I said, "Yes, but when the ball hit the ground, I blew my whistle and signaled incomplete forward pass."

McNally said, "That's right. When you blew your whistle, that 'killed the play.' Give the ball back to the Giants; place the ball on the twenty-eight-yard line. It'll be fourth down for the Giants. Now, go and announce that to the crowd."

"Announce that to the crowd?" swirled in my head. Announce to the crowd that I am taking away their touchdown and giving the ball back to the Giants? Announce not only to 67,704 in the stadium but to seventy million glued to their television sets wondering, "Well, I wonder how Tunney is gonna get out of this one?"

There is no choice in my mind—keep my poise. Just do the right thing, which is to announce just what happened. I ran to the center of the field (fifty-yard line) just in front of the Bears' bench, and faced the MNF camera. I turned on my microphone and said, "Although instant replay is ruling that play a fumble, I had blown my whistle for an incomplete forward pass. No touchdown. Giants' ball. Fourth down." I'm sure Bears' Coach Mike Ditka, although he made no overt gesture at that time, took me off his Christmas card list. The booing went on several minutes. The Giants punted (fourth down). Bears caught the punt and returned it thirteen yards. Time out for a commercial.

As I ran from one end of the field to the other—with the continued booing—I was thinking, "Was that a forward pass or was it a fumble?" (Note: I've watched that play over a hundred times and it's still hard to determine which it was). No, I was not thinking that. I was thinking: concentrate on the next play. Focus. In order to survive at that historic moment I must (1) believe in myself as a good official; (2) block out any thoughts of self-doubt; (3) not review that play in my mind; (4) focus on the task at hand; and (5) keep my poise.

That state of mind we call poise occurs when a live connection exists between your sense of yourself and your sense of purpose. This state, in all its various shadings—satisfaction, optimism, eagerness, contentment, etc.—includes every moment of solution or decision. Once you learn this and can draw upon it to quickly spot situations, you'll find that "poise" in one form or another becomes immediately more accessible to you.

People are at their best when facing challenge and adversity. I am convinced of this. There's ample proof of it in dramatic situations, like war, love, sports, and in everyday life as well. People seek to stretch themselves and to go after what they want. Unfortunately, this attribute, which gives extraordinary power when properly used, can just as powerfully be undermining in even ordinary situations if one's intelligence and potential are misused.

A hero is no braver than an ordinary man, but he is brave five minutes longer.

—Ralph Waldo Emerson

CHAPTER 7

Good Bets

You're packing a suitcase for a place none of us has been
A place that has to be believed to be seen.
—from the song "Walk On" by U2

The Jets were victorious on a cold afternoon at the Meadowlands on January 4, 2003 sending the Indianapolis Colts back to the Midwest to begin their off season. With this shutout in the first round of the 2002 playoffs—following the thorough dismantling of the Green Bay Packers the week before that put them there—the New York Jets celebrated for finding vindication in what had been widely considered a lost season. Unusual and trying as it might have been, the up-and-down campaign was never lost, not when there were still games to play and fifty-three men were still wearing the same throwback green and white jerseys. As long as there remained a present moment to fill with effort, there remained a reason to do so.

The unknown permeates all human experience. To attempt anything is to venture into areas where outcomes are uncertain and subject to variables that will fall outside the realm of our control. The only absolute exceptions to this universal law are Harlem Globetrotter games, the surety with which a Labrador retriever will rejoin a stick thrown into pounding surf and a baby creating the need for a diaper change at the most inopportune moment. These events are dependable and predictable. All else has a question mark hovering somewhere near it.

In the course of our human history the questions have become more inward and abstract, and we have managed to eliminate great fields of chance in our endeavors. Imagine how fate must have appeared to an early explorer. It wasn't that long ago—a narrow sliver of our time on the planet—that setting out by land or sea was to plunge into an unfamiliar world full of danger. Simply returning from an expedition into unknown territory was a triumphant achievement. As time went by and our skill in navigation and mapmaking developed, we began to plot the points that allowed for greater vision and direction in the physical world.

We *began* to plot the points, the implication being that the course of discovery was initiated with a single point, a central fact, and a bedrock truth. Once ancient mariners began to move away from the security of a visible coastline, their navigational skills started with a direction, moving toward or away from recognized heavenly bodies when weather conditions permitted. Dead reckoning filled in when celestial observations were impractical, the navigator making a detailed hunch based on speed, distance, and drift. Later development of tools such as the sextant allowed them to fix their positions on the open sea by deciphering degrees of latitude and longitude and finding corresponding locations on charts and maps. These degrees are also known as minutes in navigational terms. With one true minute, a navigator can set a course across the widest, deepest, and most forbidding passage.

For the Jets, the ingredients had all been there, especially after a heroic passing of the leadership baton from the aging veteran to the studious youngster at the quarterback position. But something had eluded this organization; something had those same fifty-three men searching in dark "corners" by themselves for something they would need each other to find. And find it they did, in time to make a bold investment in each other and secure their presence in the postseason. It was bigger, faster, and stronger than any single player. It was smarter and more confident than any of the coaches. It was everything they needed to escape from themselves and get back to work. And all they had to do was surrender to it.

By now, of course, we have Earth pretty well graphed. Cars with talking GPS have eliminated much of the former mystery of a journey across two states. Formerly inaccessible corners of the globe now enjoy thriving economies based on tourism, catering to people for whom exotic locations are just an e-ticket away. For better or worse we have learned to coexist with intricately programmed missiles aimed everywhere for military and political purposes. Cameras sweep most of the planet's real estate from every conceivable angle—including the bird's eye run across the width of a football field when certain networks are broadcasting NFL games.

But there is the space between points, like the distance between the sticks when the Jets are driving at the two-minute warning. Or three feet of carpet between the release of the toddler's tenacious grip on the sofa cushion and Papa's arms beckoning from the easy chair. It's where we find ourselves when the car breaks down between interstate exits. It's the tunnel of life into which teenagers disappear, the one that connects all their care and nurturing with their adult independence. It's the necessity of doing, the imperative to act that defines our existence as higher animals, prepared or not. Leaps must still be made into the unknown; in a life lived with any degree of purpose this is unavoidable. And it is then that we understand and appreciate the strength of the platform we're leaping from. Faith is a fixed point, a true minute. What we believe in is a foundation value, and it allows us to make choices and move forward with confidence in the face of risk.

Think about a competitor like Joe Namath, the former Jets quarterback and Hall of Famer, someone who earned a reputation for wading into the middle of a lost cause and, with the quickest hands, pulling out victory like it was a kitten stuck in a tree. He was supremely confident, but you never heard him boast. You never saw him beating his chest. Parenthetically, it should be noted that prior to Super Bowl III in which the Jets upset the Baltimore Colts on January 12, 1969, Joe "guaranteed" a victory. While it sounded way too boastful at that time, Joe was simply stating the confidence he had in himself and the Jets. I know Joe. He is quiet, yet completely confident. Time and again he would deliver when the chips were down, with a demeanor so calm and under control that all of the sportswriters went for angles involving supernatural intervention. There was nothing supernatural about Joe Namath. In those circumstances where he shone brightest he was propelled by belief, and that's as natural as it gets. Somewhere in him was a space reserved for certainty, the certainty that was due him for the courage of his convictions. The same can be said for another Joe—named Montana.

When Namath or Montana took the field in the closing minutes of a game that appeared to be lost, they had the power to reverse the flow of departing spectators, not to mention the flow of blitzing linebackers. Nobody wanted to miss what was going to happen. They didn't want to read about it in the paper the next morning. If fortune turned around, they wanted to savor their own impressions of the experience. The writers would talk about them as if a heavenly hand had reached down and taken over, and they'd be half right. It's the hand reaching up that delivers. It's in the seeking, not the hoping, where the power and the confidence are found. Their core beliefs, the source of their inner strength and extraordinary composure, are that they sought something bigger than themselves.

Coach Edwards observes, "I can tell when our team has that confidence working. They look a little lighter, they move a little quicker, and their energy is steady, with no peaks and valleys to fall from or climb out of. We've arrived. We're here. Fear has no place in this state of preparation, and the absence of the morale killer gives everyone a winning rhythm. This looks like a swagger, if exhibited by a group of players who are self-involved. But, among a group of guys dedicated to each other, the rhythm is the dance of success. The deal is—I often tell the team—you play to win the game!"

In the locker room, following their victory over the Colts away from the tumult of an overflowing and adoring crowd, the Jets' players and coaches gathered in close. Coach Edwards's remarks were spare and forthright, only loud enough to reach the outer edge of this satisfied company. When he finished a short address, the players took a knee and made some sort of contact with each other. Behemoth men with clumps of turf still hanging from their seams and crevices reach out with stepped-on fingers and bruised forearms to touch each other. Hands on each other's sweaty necks, resting on jersey numbers, covering battered knees, they heed their coach's request. It gets quiet. Nothing is happening. Everything is happening. What's already done is done. What awaits them is unknown. But here they are, now, where it matters most. Somebody—not the coach—offers up a prayer.

"The suspense is terrible. I hope it will last," uttered the Irish writer Oscar Wilde in a thoroughly human homage to uncertainty. There may be great apprehension about how something is going to turn out, yet we seek the risk and face the unknown with primal obedience. Why? Because there is little doubt that when we are confronted with this state of mind we are highly alert and most alive. The mind, by its very nature, is a goal-setting machine. It envisions goals just as naturally as the body seeks movement, and both get achy if held quiet too long. Adventurers—the sort of people who blaze routes up unscaled mountains or attempt to circumnavigate the planet in hot-air balloons—are quick to point out the invigorating effects of taking chances. Life "on the edge" describes an exhilaration derived from our encounters with stress.

One doesn't have to look for sheer rock faces above the tree line to find the arena of chance. In everyday life there are actions we take and decisions we make that move us out toward the edge, where we have the opportunity to wager something of ourselves, to enliven the way. Imagine—or remember—that first plunge off the high dive and what it means to the youngster standing there at the very edge of the atmosphere wondering whether gravity will turn out to be friend or foe. Picture a middle-aged woman in physical therapy, after recovering from an accident, making up her mind about advancing from walking to running on the treadmill. It's something she hasn't done since she was a child, and a small part of her brain is still telling her that it isn't a possibility. Or put yourself in the place of the guy who has to stand up in front of a large audience and convince them of something, to persuade them to move to a new understanding of some issue, sweaty palms, shallow breath, and all.

The challenges are constant, and we are always heading for them whether we like it or not. Sometimes our goals are clearly defined, by design and by necessity. Other times we find ourselves moving from known Point A to unknown Point B for the heck of it, or, as a famous mountaineer once put it when somebody asked him why he wanted to climb a particular peak, "Because it is there." This movement toward the unrevealed result is simply part of living. Animals don't make such a big deal out of it. But along with our human power of reasoning comes the ability to project and anticipate, both positively and negatively. The pressure starts building in our bigger brains.

When a T*E*A*M is preparing for a game, a lot of elements need to merge into one atmosphere of readiness. They take care of those elements that seem to have broken down during the week, when they can be methodical, deliberate, and specific. Come Sunday, the team gathers to be collected at the edge. They want to possess an "edge." An air of being confident and anxious, stressed into a state of mind that can be described as "accelerated calm." It is in this state of mind that their best work is done as a football team.

There are many different ways of finding that acceleration, but there is only one way to find the calm. If there is no trust in each other, or in the certainty of one good effort leading to another, a team will never be composed enough to do what needs to be done. If there is no faith in the positive outcome that follows preparation and effort, the confidence won't be there. If there is no belief in something that can't necessarily be seen, the suitcase for the trip will never get packed.

All of this leaping into the unknown begs the question of whether unnecessary risks are being taken. Is the thrill the product of mere chance? For some people, fate is really no more than that, a roll of the dice. But talk to someone who makes a living in a dangerous occupation, and chances are very good that behind the observable peril is diligent preparation, a systematic attempt to minimize the risks involved. Racecar drivers never fail to buckle seat belts—even when it's a short trip out for a loaf of bread in the family car. A fireman is anything but reckless as he probes for openings in the physical chess game he plays with a burning building, relying on his training to reveal the correct moves. Skydivers with long resumes share the habit of meticulously packing their own chutes and checking all their own hardware, so that doubt is not riding piggyback during an earthward plunge ninety miles per hour. Unless a martyr syndrome compels us, one of the ways we measure success is by surviving. There's a daily form of heroism in simply continuing to show up—for any job (regardless of the risk factors), for school, for family, for belief. This continuity requires preparation, some prior commitment to sensibly handling the risks involved.

The post-game prayer in the locker room is no bald appeal for the Maker to become the free safety, the offensive coordinator, or the water boy on a team bound for success. Nobody is demanding that God make those guys the last men standing in the war for the championship trophy. The words are simple and spontaneously humble, spoken by a man just given the opportunity to earn his keep working in the turf while a crowd watches. His teammates murmur their assent, and even if the beliefs held in the room vary from man to man, they are here united as they recognize something outside themselves, as they seek a common, binding truth. Good football is a natural by-product of this rugged submission. And the more they give it up, the better the football gets.

Few may face life-or-death circumstances each day, and very few get to play professional football. But each of us grapples with the unknown on some level. We arrive at points of departure from what is predictable or comfortably known. We all want there to be dependable bridges leading from those points to where we want to go. As noted, these challenging points have tended to take on a more inward aspect as the physical world has come under greater and greater control. It has become more the stuff of our inner selves. Dwight Morrow zeroed in on this fact when he remarked, "What lies behind us and what lies before us are tiny matters compared to what lies within us." Somewhere within us we need to have one true minute stored.

Mike Chapman a lifelong friend of Edwards, says, "I never think of Herman as someone who takes risks," fully recognizing as he explains this that risk is inescapable, in either his or anybody else's life. "Herman's deal is you work hard, you do the right thing, and good things are going to happen. That spirit is going to take care of him and guide him," Mike continues. This constitutes quite a tribute to both the depth and the humility of Edwards's faith and spiritual center. When we think of doing something with no risk, two possible scenarios leap to mind: either we are utterly ignorant of the reality of a situation ("Sure, I'll buy some of that swampland, since you tell me the gators down there are tame enough to eat right out of your hand") or that the circumstance is so predictable that it has been rendered dull. It's tantalizing to think that a third possibility might be some divine magic made available to us in the exercise of faith without preparation or responsibility.

But such a quid pro quo is a false one, a fantasy that places more of the responsibility for how things turn out on the creator or supervising entity of our choice, and less on us. We can and should prepare ourselves for whatever challenge or mission we face. It's our job to do that. We're responsible for what lies on this side of the line of control. Yet the finished product of our preparation is greatly enhanced when something fills the void lying beyond what Abraham Lincoln called "our poor power to add or detract." In the speech from which those words emerged, he asserted that we have no right to deify ourselves, and that our actions and sacrifices—as with the soldiers at Gettysburg—speak more clearly about our character than does our wishful thinking.

Chapman speaks of the "deal," and it would seem an excellent choice of words. Because then the stipulation is that "you work hard, you do the right thing, and good things are going to happen," is a quid pro quo worth investing in. It has been a cornerstone of Herm's character since the lessons in life given by his father, yet he does not make a spectacle of these personal beliefs. He believes he must show them to you, that is, "walk my talk." Preferring to put faith in motion and to allow the world to judge the results of his actions rather than relying on the superficial effect of mere words.

What Edwards's dad was teaching him and what he learned early was that if he was afraid to fail, then he would never succeed ("Don't be afraid of the broom"). As an athlete, he really understood it, and he started living his life that way. Filling in blank pages through faith and finding liberation in the idea that hard work would be met with guiding hands, he learned that fear of failure had no business in the life of someone who recognized a higher source. Edwards doesn't need to stand on a pulpit. He believes there are a lot of ways to profess ones beliefs. For him, it's simply how he acts, how he lives his life. It's personal. But when people ask, he is not shy in telling them. There are lots of ways that God uses you, and you just have to understand the way you'll be employed. And once you understand that, you have to commit your life to living it that way.

It's probably harder being a head coach, because you really open yourself up to ridicule. People examine you—you, not your strategy, or the people you hired, or your coaching tendencies—and they'll say, "Hey, this guy professes to be this or that, and I just saw him do this other thing. He's not what he says he is." In what Coach Edwards does for a living, he's on a stage—in a fishbowl. He likes that pressure: he believes consistency is strength, and he depends on it. When others look at Herm, maybe see something a little different and wonder how he does it, they wonder what motivates him.

Herm says, "If they get inquisitive and ask, I tell them. I like it on that basis. If you go around talking all the time, bringing all this attention to whatever is going on in your head, you're apt to start thinking you can handle everything. That's not a desirable state of mind. When you think you've got it all figured out, you're in for trouble. There are going to be things you can't handle. And that's when you want to know you've got some backup."

Gifts are part of the "deal," part of the mystery of life that we can find our way into with faith. There is no clear reason why some people have the innate talent or physical structure to perform certain physical tasks while others don't. Or why some people possess the mental tools to achieve in ways that others can't. It's all part of the world of unknown possibilities. What is clear is that each of us is empowered to do something well. If we accept responsibility for the care and upkeep of that gift, then we accept some form of its divine distribution. Gifts are like messages sent saying there is a connection between the world of our control and the one beyond. There it is. Take it.

It's yours to use for a little while.

Trust is the transmitter. Trust is faith's twin brother. If we trust the origin of whatever gift we possess, then we can be confident in its use—but only if we have honored it with hard work and preparation. That trust is passed along in a chain of belief that has to remain intact. Effective leadership is not achieved just because a leader has found the means to make other people submit to what he wants. Effective leadership eliminates, with trust, the barriers between a message sent and a message received.

In a group situation such as a professional football team, there has to be a supervising vision. Coach Edwards has experienced this from several different perspectives and knows what he's talking about. There has to be one voice that sets the tone at the end of the day. It's his role to lead. The players perform. He feels he is no more superior to them than a doctor is to a clergyman. Every role is exalted. Every role is vital. The coach or leader is not the craftsman shaping the door but the leader who has to make sure that the hinges are put where they need to be and to see to it that they don't fail. It's a big old door, and the smallest thing on it is the hinge. Somebody has to make sure that the good work done on the hinges is a match with the doorjamb and that the jamb is a good match with the header. That supervising vision is to see the whole door as the unified sum of its parts. Again, Herman Sr. was an important teacher in that respect. He always urged his son to believe in what he was doing and not let other people distract him from the vision he had created.

If the leader has no vision, it's going to be a hard road for those following. The leader has to be able to alleviate the intimidation of difficult circumstances and stay focused on the desire and prepared for result. During the football season, the vision is to win each game, one game at a time. It is very simple, not very hard at all. A nice, clear vision: win one. But with a lot of people involved and a lot of different elements and ingredients thrown into the mix, it can get complex. So the coach's job is to find that simplicity and help others focus on that same thing. The coach is the shield, and he fights to nullify the distractions that a team may be experiencing. If he's erasing the distractions, then there had better be something worth believing in to take its place.

When you think about that chain of trust, there is perhaps no more dramatic illustration of it than a jet-fighter squadron. One flyer leads, and each following pilot takes his positioning cue from the wing in front of him. At mach 1, that's an extraordinary leap of faith and trust. There can be no room for doubt, no second-guessing. If the leader's vision and judgment is sound, then the trust allows for surrender to the greater good, the bigger picture, and the confidence that this group of supersonic machines is going to function as a single unit and come home safely. But if that chain of trust is broken for whatever reason, everybody is scrambling out of control. Everybody can't lead. There has to be a supervising vision worth the surrender that must be made to it. That's the leader's responsibility. With intelligence and hard work, a leader can open his or her arms wide to uncertainty and lead people with confidence. That's Coach Edwards's job—his "deal."

Chapman continues, "Herman's steadiness as a person and coach has a prismatic quality. The light he throws is no more or less than the light he has gathered from the course of his own inspiration. It is very important to him that the actions his messages send remain constant and uncorrupted. He recognizes that in a leadership role, his stability of character is not an optional feature; the clear direction of the group requires it." If players say, "Coach is coming out of character," that's when you lose the team. If you are the head guy and you show them your will, they say, "Coach is okay. If he's okay, we're okay." If you let everyone influence you, they become the coach. You always have to remember, you're the coach. This is your team. You have to do it the way you see fit. Your vision is your vision.

We need not recede from our own thoughts, dreams, and impressions about the world of our choosing. We don't have to stand in envy of the people with "vision." Creative visualization—a concept that encourages people to see the precise dimensions of the goal they are striving for—is old-hat stuff to people of faith. A willingness to vacate our own egos and believe in the guidance of something outside ourselves is the foundation of this spiritual state—no robes, candles, or incantations necessary. To believe in one's own ability, given the opportunity and careful preparation, is to add another component to the personal system we build in pursuit of our vision. Extending this confidence to family, to friends, to teammates and coworkers, is a veritable act of worship.

Coach stands in the light of his beliefs and reflect its goodness down the road. That's what Edwards means when he says it's just how he lives his life, period. It's how he treats people and conducts himself. It's all wrapped around his faith. Mike Chapman continues, "There is a tone of modest self-assurance, the understated chutzpah that swirls through Herman's character and runs out of him in a river of energy that pushes high along the banks but never floods." How big a role does faith play in Herm's life? His wife, Lia, says, "Faith is huge. There is faith in himself, yes, and in family, and it gets its meaning from his faith in God. His personal belief is not dry and abstract. It's active, and it works hard. He knows how to bestow those values on his team so that they can play as a team. The players pay him a real compliment when they describe him as being the same at the beginning and at the end of the season. He keeps the same philosophy. He is the same man, built on his beliefs, rooted in his faith."

Which may just be, in the final analysis, a hereditary trait. Or as Chapman explains: "I was talking to Martha [Herman's mother], and we got around to the subject of music. I was asking her what kind of music she liked, and she told me that when she was pregnant with Herman she used to listen to Liberace. She would listen to Liberace and pray that her baby would be famous. And I told her, 'You know, I hope you remember those prayers, and I hope you still have your Liberace collection, because I think I might have to start listening to Liberace and praying those same prayers." Her prayers are being answered.

The Official's Call

It's often quiet in the official's locker room prior to game time. While in each team's locker room there is music—often loud—or the obvious headphones on each player as he develops his own form of meditation, each player has perhaps a different way of mental preparation. And so does each official.

In the locker room some study the rulebook. Occasionally, a "wag" will venture forth with a not-so-bright comment, "If you don't know the rules by now, it's too late." Wrong! It's never too late to remind oneself of the correct rule. The rules are intricate at best, and a quick review sets ones mind on alert stage.

As an example, before each game I would remind our crew to "get the kickoff right." If the game starts with an error in rules interpretation, the whole day (re: game) seems out of whack. Just a simple play on the kickoff where the kicking team (Team A) kicks the ball more than ten yards, the receiving team (Team B) touches the ball, so a Team A player (called A1) picks up the ball and runs for a touchdown. If the line judge sees A1 pick up the ball and run for an apparent touchdown, then trails A1 and signals "touchdown," we have a problem. Team A cannot run with a kickoff unless a Team B player possess the ball and then fumbles it. Team A will get the ball at the spot A1 picked it up, but there is no touchdown.

The stadium crowd of seventy-five-thousand-plus and x millions watching on the television is confused. If there's no touchdown, then why did the line judge signal touchdown? Many reasons. The most apparent is that the line judge didn't "remind" himself that Team A cannot advance a kicked ball on a kickoff unless Team B possesses and then fumbles: Rule 6, Section 2, Article 26, page 36. Simple. The NFL rulebook has 112 pages of rules that need to be learned and constantly reviewed.

"Walk your talk" or "above reproach," whatever the phrase, NFL officials must demonstrate by their example that no outside influence will affect their judgment. If one fan or a stadium full of fans believes that an official is dishonest, then all is lost. Maybe a better word is "perceived" to be dishonest. It is as important to live as honest a life off the field as on the field.

I was speaking to a Fortune 500 company in Las Vegas late in my officiating career and was walking through the casino of the hotel where the convention was being held with the CEO of the company. As we approached the casino, I quietly removed my Super Bowl ring. The CEO noticed this slight-of-hand and said, "Why did you do that?"

I said, "Perception. Someone may recognize me [I'm still surprised how often that happens.] and think to himself, 'Looks like officials gamble. I wonder if they bet on games.'" I can't take that chance and place all officials and the game in jeopardy.

Cuz, We're on a Mission, Baby!

*If a man wants to be of the greatest possible value to
his fellow creatures, let him begin the long, solitary
task of perfecting himself.*

—Robertson Davies

There are very few subjects that will coax the latent silence out of Edwards's good friend, former coach, and mentor, Dick Vermeil. His natural gregariousness fills his immediate environment with a flow of words that engages, prods, and enlightens. His professional reputation is anchored on a verbal talent that always manages to find the words that a given situation calls for. Nobody who knows him would ever label him a ham, though the shaking heads might turn to nods if the description was upgraded to preacher. The man can present.

But try to lure him into self-admiration and you'll be left holding the microphone. Attempt to flush out any suggestion of vanity and you'll find the fountain of words has dried up. He won't grandstand about the contributions he's made, either to the world of sport or to the world at large. Personal displays of his achievements are not part of his repertoire. On that particular subject, Vermeil has little to say—and everything to do.

He'll be his talkative self in pursuit of you, if there is some contribution you might make that has not already been tallied. It doesn't matter what that contribution is. And though he'd love to see you putting time or money into the projects undertaken by his favorite cause, he'd be the first to inform you that it's not necessary to stand in line at his tent, under his banner, tossing nickels and dimes into his pot, to make a difference. It's not a matter of prestige, or politics, or appearances—habits that may be tough to root out of our motives if they've been there for long—but you need to go somewhere.

Your open heart or your agile mind or your helping hands are the missing ingredients in some scenario where those who can are paving the way for those who haven't yet had the chance. As Bob Dylan once belted out in a song, with the excitement of someone who has just found undeniable proof that the world is round, not flat: "You've got to serve somebody!" To give honestly and generously of one's energy and talents is to lift the gift from its cradle and go worldwide with it. We see. We feel. We contribute. Each such contribution gets life from all the others made. And in that sense, you'll end up putting something into Dick Vermeil's pot regardless—just as he has given to yours.

Edwards strives to live up to that example during the annual youth football camp in Monterey. Each year Edwards has been fortunate enough to collect a Who's Who list of current and former NFL players and coaches as instructors and motivators, and the results have been extraordinarily gratifying. The atmosphere is high energy and hopeful, bursting with an enthusiasm for good things to happen that unites all the participants. On any given day this enthusiasm might first be noticed in someone like the founder (Edwards) striding the fields at California State University, Monterey Bay, located in Seaside, California and plunking litter into a bag. Or it might be seen also in someone like Joe Bommarito, camp director, who, after helping police the empty fields, goes over the schedule for the day, inspiring the camp's volunteers to face the daily invasion of eager young people. All of the camp's personnel are volunteers; they number about sixty-plus. And at any point during the camp's instructional periods, the enthusiasm might show up in a pro football player on the field backpedaling, helpless to resist demonstrating what he knows to a budding generation of coverage guys.

Clay Larson is another of the fine men on whom Herman depends to continue serving youth. A Monterey bank president and civic leader, Larson's been a staunch supporter of all Edwards's outreach efforts. Clay observes, "Herman absolutely leads by example. It's tough to keep up with him. It's tough to keep up with his level of energy and organization, with his passion. And it is a passion. A passion to do the right thing."

Herm is undoubtedly backpedaling in the face of such praise. Clay already had gone the extra mile on Herm's behalf. Back in the early 1980s, Larson sponsored Edwards for membership at the Pacheco Club in Monterey, an exclusive retreat for local business-men. Herm was the club's first prospective black member, and Clay took some heat for that. Older club members were wondering if what Clay was proposing was really in the best interests of the club. Clay stuck with it because he believed in what Herman might bring to the organization. It was a struggle, and some members didn't buy into the change for some time, but Clay's vision of a motivated and inte-grated group of business professionals was stronger than their resist-ance. He's already provided an example worth following to all the others whose contributions have become part of the chain of reciprocal giving.

Gut Check

A young dad leans over The Youth Foundation's registration table, signing up his nine-year-old boy for the football camp. The cheerful-ness that comes with this task has other moms and dads bobbing their heads up and down to join in the group conversation while they jot down information on their forms. The dad is saying hello and trading quips with everybody, even those he's never spoken to before. He looks up from his own paperwork to make eye contact with someone who has just paid his son a compliment as an athlete, and notices a near-by table with a placard marked "COACHES." He tears a check out of his checkbook, hands it over, and waves as he walks away, glowing a little bit from the unsolicited recognition just given to his son.

His son is a good player and a fine boy—he's watched him grow and develop for a couple of seasons now, and the dad enjoys the warm feeling that these are his sweet days of boyhood in a setting better than the one he grew up in. His son has found a game of touch with a handful of other fourth graders, and their catcalls fill the cool morning air. Dad gives him the high wave (meaning "Gotta go now") with the thumb jerk (meaning "before Mom gets mad") that pulls his laughing offspring away from the impromptu game. As he watches his son run across the field to him, an impulse that has been building in him takes over his feet, spins him around, and sends him back to the second table where its clipboarded list is flapping in the breeze. There his son catches up to him.

"What are you doing, Dad? Didn't you sign me up?"

"I did. I did. But now I have to sign me up."

"For what?"

"On this list here."

*The boy leans over, flattens the waving sheet and reads out loud:
"Coaching sign-up list." He looks at his father. "You mean you're
gonna . . ."*

"Well, let's—let's see it. What do you say?"

*The boy processes the information for a moment, and then
exhibits an excited expression like an explorer falling into a won-
drous hidden cave.*

*"I'm gonna go tell . . ." And he takes off running, his tangled legs
barely able to keep up with the rest of him. Ten yards later, he stops
with a screech and turns around. "Hey, Dad—am I gonna be a wide
receiver?" he wonders gravely.*

*"We'll see," replies the dad, already working on the diplomacy
that will become an integral part of the job.*

There is a reason why people step lightly in the presence of mentors. You'll see that when a CEO returns to his thirtieth school
reunion, lingering respectfully in the doorway before greeting the old
man in the bow tie who taught him how to begin expressing his opin-
ions with good grammar. It's the polite excitement that a professional
musician shows when handing over her orchestra's latest CD to the
slender woman who showed her how to make the cello come alive in
the fifth grade. It's the spin-away maneuver and the quick, easy grin
struck between the mailman and the math teacher who also worked
with the receivers on the junior varsity team way back when. The
time taken in the present, the energy donated in the here and now,
produces huge future dividends in the lives of the recipients and the
donors. These gifts echo on and on through time. The lessons are
open-ended transactions with no closing dates.

At Highland School, an elementary school, there was a man
there by the name of Mr. Vaughn. Everybody knew who Mr. Vaughn
was. If you were acting up on the playground, he'd clunk your heads
together and convince you that, despite your talented jive or your
boxing moves, he was going to maintain a more dignified atmosphere than the one you were advocating. No one was running around
in fear of Mr. Vaughn; people were running around in respect of
him. There were some other fellows from Edwards's early days who
played similar roles in the lives of Seaside kids. There was Billy

DeBarry, a middle-school principal at Martin Luther King School, who later became Herm's counselor at Monterey High. There was a man named Carl Stevenson, Herm's physical education teacher at MLK middle school, who ended up coaching football at Seaside High.

Reflecting on the relationships that Herm had with those men, it all feels like the present tense. It feels like he merely stepped away for a while and has lessons and concerns yet to learn and discuss with them, that there are examples remaining to be set and to be followed. They were a vital part of growing up. They gave kids some discipline and made sure they acted right. Someone like that, whether it's a father or someone like Mr. Vaughn, or maybe a father and another role model working independently of each other but on parallel tracks, will be a continuous presence in the life of a kid as he or she grows and develops. They will help establish the lineage of passing on values and experience, and they will place the young person into a context of personal responsibility.

Gut Check

There was this housepainter who hadn't worked in several weeks, and was lamenting all the free time he'd been spending at home. These lulls in his work schedule during the rainy winter months were beginning to take an unreasonable toll on him. He felt like a football lineman in a perpetual three-point stance, frozen in the ready position and unable to relax. For the past several mornings his professional life had consisted of aimless wandering on the internet with a coffee cup in his hand, followed by an hour or two of phone calls to people who hadn't developed any new work for him since the last time he contacted them. His business was cyclical, and sometimes there was nothing to do but hang on until he was back on the upswing. His faith was durable enough to weather the stormy season, but there was the question of how to fill the time that he felt should be spent in some kind of productive labor.

A bright orange sheet of paper caught his eye from the middle of the stack of bills on the back of his desk. Hoping it wasn't an exotic overdue notice—it would almost certainly mean that some vital service was hours away from disconnection—he pulled it out and looked at it. It was a notice from his child's teacher, explaining that the class was launching into a production that would require as much outside assistance as she could muster. The show needed a

*costume person, a choreographer, and a set designer in particular.
He was a big fan of his daughter's elementary theatre projects and
had attended several of them with enjoyment and great respect for
the commitment to the cause he saw in the youngsters. Yet he'd
always assumed that these things just sort of happened, that they
were created in the domain of housewives who came home with
classroom paste sticking to their fingers. The school volunteer stuff
was alien to him.*

*But the notice was speaking directly to him. There was no doubt
that his expertise could be put to effective use; all of the theatre sets
he'd seen so far had consisted mainly of great sheets of craft paper
turned into murals with the bold application of tempera paint. Paint,
he could do. An idea or two popped into his head about how to wind
the fabled yellow brick road through Room 28. As he thought about
it some more, he remembered some canvas drop cloths that were left
over from his last job. Stretch those over some two-by-two wood, and
it would be easy to make some panels that would be far easier both
to paint and to maneuver on and off the stage during set changes ...*

*Three weeks later he woke up with butterflies in his stomach for
the first time in years. The show was going on that day, and everybody wanted it to be perfect. It was well rehearsed, and it looked
great. His set-design job had expanded to include special effects,
sound, and lights, and anything else that the teacher had thrown at
him in the race to prepare the play. He found a profound sense of
connection with these kids, and he knew that he was, for the life of
the show, a vital player in the drama of their young lives. It was an
indescribably good feeling. Small matter that when the "real world"
painting jobs began to return, he'd had to arrange a few workdays
around the rehearsal schedule. The show had to go on. That's all
there was to it. And it did. The housepainter's volunteer efforts made
it happen.*

Before Herm Edwards was offered the job with the Jets, he met
with several individuals within the organization and was assessed on
many levels. He welcomed this close examination, this thorough evaluation of who he is and what he stands for. Jets owner Robert Wood
Johnson IV, or "Woody," as he is more commonly referred to, played
an important role in that process. Johnson spent many hours talking
and exploring areas of mutual interest and found deep agreement on

several principles with Herm. Foremost among these is the idea that football must be played and life must be lived beyond the confines of the ego. Johnson credits Edwards with the statement, "You play for the NFL, you play for the game. You play for the history of the game and for all of the people who have ever played the game. It's not for the name on the back of the jersey; it's for the logo on the helmet."

Edwards can also credit his owner with the creation of an atmosphere in which personal integrity and the honor of the game are encouraged and rewarded. Johnson understands very well that in an era of such inflated hype and money surrounding professional sport, if the honor of the game is not upheld, then the game loses. The game goes downhill, and we're left with a cult of personalities paid to wear the colors of a particular town only until a fatter envelope obliges them to go somewhere else.

Edwards's pride comes out this way, "An organization that puts such a premium on selflessness, starting right at the top with the owner is the one I want to work for. I may be the more visible symbol of the Jets' management, but I am not the lord and master of this club. I am one link in the chain, and I have a job to do. It requires that I assert my ideas and standards in a vigorous way on a daily basis, but I only have to look at the Jets' AFC East Divisional Championship trophy to remember that I have the privilege of serving a tradition that is greater than I am."

Before Edwards was hired his views were well aired around the Jets' complex. In addition to Woody Johnson, Herm spoke extensively with Terry Bradway, the general manager. They had known each other during earlier days at the Kansas City Chiefs and had found common ground to re-explore in a new way. They talked about being in focus and paying attention to details. "Ya gotta get the corners," Herm reminded himself as his father's words rang loud and clear. They talked about schedules, and a bottom-line philosophy about being on time and being accountable. They formulated the question that every player should ask himself after every practice, after every game, and after every public appearance: "What did I do to make the game better?"

This question does not refer strictly to Xs and Os, or to the simple accumulation of statistics. It does not confine itself to the results of a single afternoon but to the shape of the game as an ongoing enterprise. It recognizes that the nature of one's contribution may change due to circumstances, but it insists that there is always a contribution to be made. Edwards believes that the most important thing we do in life is to be givers rather than takers, whether we're talking about membership on a football team, or membership in the human community. You've got to give something back. Much has been given to you—life, liberty, the opportunity to succeed—and you've got to give something back. That is how accomplishments are truly celebrated.

Joe Bommarito and Mike Chapman are bedrock contributors to The Youth Foundation with their time, energy, and wisdom. The effort they put into the football camp and its related activities each year as volunteers would represent fulltime jobs for many people, but they've been returning year after year because for each man it is his nature, and also his habit, to give back, to make himself an instrument of help. Their contributions began back in the 1980s in the Monterey area.

As Edwards's playing career came to a close, he was spending more time back home and was reconnecting with people and institutions from earlier periods in his life.

Bommarito had played at Fresno State, and returned to become a coach at MPC. Chapman attended MPC and became a professional golf teacher and continues to do so today. These fellows became great natural resources in reacquainting Herm with the community. He became—again—involved with the old Boys Club in Seaside, where he had spent so much time as a kid. The club was struggling. The building was getting old, was too small, and fresh air needed to be breathed into the program that had been such a touchstone for so many kids. Serving on the board of directors, Herm's enthusiasm persuaded Chapman to join in helping put "new life" into the club, which Mike was glad to do because he was also a Boys Club alumnus. In the early days, it was called the Boys Club. The name was changed in 1989 to include all young people. The name today is the Boys and Girls Clubs of Monterey County. Wow! How it has grown!

Edwards and his friends began to fund raise and initiate improvement projects, but after a while Herm found that they could work best independent of the sitting board of directors. Thus, The Youth Foundation was formed. They initiated an annual charity golf tournament, donations from which became the building fund for the Boys and Girls Club, and for whatever other purposes The Youth

Foundation earmarked it. The Youth Foundation grew and developed, at first in parallel with the Boys and Girls Club, and then widening to include other outreach projects not part of the club's purview. "Team Edwards" became a blur around the Monterey Peninsula, rushing here and there like Mercury or the Flash jangling their tin cup, looking for money to be spent on kids. The "team" had some pretty fit current and former athletes on board, and nobody could outrun them. They were, indeed, "on a mission."

Mike Chapman describes these early fundraising efforts this way: "Herman would come home from his NFL playing or coaching days and do the golf tournament that turned him slightly maniacal. He'd have a couple of weeks vacation, and he'd hit the ground running. He'd say, 'Here's what we gotta do.' I'd take some time off from my golf teaching and we'd jump in the car and drive around as if at any moment the ground would open up and swallow all the donors, if we didn't get to them first. We'd go 'bang up' on everybody we knew. For a hundred bucks. It was always a hundred bucks. Herman would always say, 'Get us a hundred bucks,' and, man, everybody will give ya a hundred bucks."

"So we would go and badger everybody we knew for a Ben Franklin. I remember one time pulling over off the street and right up onto the sidewalk for an unscheduled meeting with a couple of guys that Herman knew. He didn't even get out of the car. He worked them from the driver's seat, and when he was done he had two hundred bucks. He looked over at me and said 'Cuz, we're on a mission, baby.' It was like that. Wherever we went the parking spots would open up, people would be in the right mood, the sun would jump out from behind a cloud. Herman was always saying 'When we're doing the right thing, good things are going to happen.' And that was pretty much the MO. 'Here's what we gotta do,' he kept saying. And everything would fall into place."

Herm admits to a certain "missionary" sense of purpose when it comes to serving these kids. It always puts a few more minutes into every hour and a couple more gallons in the gas tank. It's a liberating state of mind, and it makes it possible to overcome almost any inhibition about separating people from their money, or their free time, or their cozy notions that all this stuff happens in somebody else's department. His friends and co-conspirators are equally guilty. Joe Bommarito said, "My parents raised me to reach back and lend a hand." This golf tournament was a natural fit. Coach Phillips and Coach Pappas were involved in it from early on, and they said, "You'd better take a look at this. This is something worthwhile." They were right. And once you're in, you're in—ya know "that's the deal."

The football camp started somewhere around the eighth year of the golf tournament. The idea sprang up—why don't we do a football camp, since it's the best common denominator? The first time The Youth Foundation (TYF) had its football camp, there were about a hundred kids and a handful of volunteers. Now it's grown to the point where the kids look like Roman legions out there. And lots of volunteers. Local people, professional football players, you name it. Everybody loves it. It's become like a vacation to them. Everybody's involved, and they plan their schedules around it. And they all get an exceptionally good feeling of working with young people and giving something back. As camp director, Bommarito says, "If you took a picture of Herman on the field with the Chiefs and you took another picture of Herman on the field here at the TYF football camp, you couldn't tell the difference. Same guy, same passion, same message. That's how important it is. Our 2007 football camp held in July had eight hundred kids and eighty plus volunteers."

Gut Check

A lady rides the short distance from her office to the blood bank on a city bus during her lunch break. She's come so often the registration process is almost a reflex, but she still reads the diseases on the checklist very carefully to make sure that she's still a good candidate to give. Maybe they've discovered some new hidden danger in the molecules of a childhood microbe that kept her home from school. She flinches a little bit when they take the blood sample from her fingertip to check for anemia, but there is a smile on her face, as if she's waiting for the child she knows is hiding in the closet to leap out and yell "Boo!" It's the timing of it, not the pain.

The rest of it is clinical and ordinary, helped along by the Red Cross technicians who ask friendly questions in staccato voices as they dart from station to station securing connections and scrutinizing the slowly filling polyethylene bags. Her answers inform them that her two grown children are doing just fine, and that yes, she is still seeing her bird-watching gentleman friend. The lady learns that

Arturo just bought a new car, though not the one that his girlfriend wanted him to get. She hears a full report of a new movie from Sandra and Janet, who left the kids with their dads and managed a girls' night out. She squeezes a ball of gauze every five seconds, gently, just like they asked her to, to maintain a steady flow of her donated blood.

As she surveys the by-now familiar pattern of the acoustical ceiling tile and imagines it to be an ancient map of the world, she feels anything but heroic or exemplary. It's just something she does, and it's easy. It's the least she can do, she figures, since blood from a roomful of strangers saved her mother's life after an emergency hysterectomy so many years ago. It kept her alive, preserved her family, and gave them all more of the time they deserved together. So she pumps the gauze in her fist, hums a tune she heard on the radio, and looks forward to the cup of juice and the cookie awaiting her once her blood bag has been filled. The same nice man is volunteering again today, keeping the "recovery" table lively with his jokes and comments about the state of things.

The lady hums her tune in rhythm with the swishing sound of the blood collector and matches that small symphony with the voice of the volunteer man and the bustling choreography of the nurses attending the donors. She is alert and peaceful, and smiles slightly at how this peace can flow out of her, out of them, out of this day, out of this life. She never doubts humanity from this perspective. The remainder of the day is going to be busy with tasks she's not looking forward to, but that doesn't matter so much. The nice man at the table will offer her a T-shirt as a gesture of the Red Cross's appreciation for her coming in, but she'll turn it down. She'll leave here in another fifteen minutes thinking of her mother and feeling content and that, she figures, is all the reward that anyone needs. She was on a mission, baby.

Mrs. Edwards, Lia, is a lovely and talented person who probably never figured that she would be the wife of an NFL head coach. Perhaps that is due to the fact that in her professional life she worked for the NCAA and got to know a few coaches in the course of her job. Maybe something about the rigors of a coach's life, with the constant overtime, the travel, and the pressure to win, convinced her that such a man would not be an ideal mate. Herm's grateful she was willing to reevaluate that opinion.

When they married, she joined the high-profile world that accounts for so much of a coach's life and time; she had to make a tough transition. Suddenly she was in the public eye in a way she'd never been before, and not in the furtherance of her own career but as a companion in the world of professional football. To her enormous credit, she does not consider the change in her life to have been a sacrifice. The way she has stepped into the role of a "coach's wife" deepens the already-great respect Herm has for her. There is nothing timid about the sense of responsibility she brings to that role. The same is true for all of the other spouses in the Jets' extended family. Side by side with Lia, they have become a significant social movement, finding ways to be involved in the community that are a constant source of inspiration for the rest of us.

In New York, Lia, working with the Jets' media relations department, has organized an association of the players' and coaches' wives. Their function is to serve the community, which they do so energetically. One evening you'll find them hosting a holiday party for victims of domestic violence and their children. The next day, the woman in the Jets cap ringing the bell for the Salvation Army might be the fiancée of last year's third-round draft pick. At any time, folks lining up for a hot meal at one of the city's numerous relief centers might be breaking bread with others in the Jets' organization. As Lia describes it, the assumption is to be involved, to consider such service to be the norm and not the extracurricular exception. "It's an avenue to get involved," she says. "You can be as involved as you want. You can participate in one event or seven events. We don't make it mandatory, but by creating the opportunity, we find that good people will make it an obligation for themselves. Then it's self-directed, with each person working to satisfy an inner standard rather than one that is imposed. That's when it works best."

People think of the Jets as their local team, and that's exactly what they have—a local team. Anybody in New York who has been present at some outreach effort might have been elbow to elbow with members of the Jets' family. The way to become familiar with this group is not necessarily to line up for autographs as they emerge from the stadium tunnel but to go where they go in the community that they are a part of, helping out when they can. Many of the Jets families, along with other New Yorkers, did that in the aftermath of the 2001 9/11 attack at the World Trade Center. An empathetic urge to act in response to such cruelty drew the Jets family out in great numbers, and for the right reasons. In that horrible, sorrowful time there was no dividing line, no "us" and no "them" with regard to Jets' community relations. All citizens, brothers and sisters, united to take care of each other. It was an extreme condition of the spirit that was needed to access on a regular basis. They responded—and are still responding—admirably to a cataclysmic event.

Edwards emphasizes, "We need to continue answering that call to service. If we stop empathizing, we lose our most important frame of reference. The Golden Rule is truly a no-brainer: Do unto others as you would have them do unto you. Who doesn't want to be treated that way?" Conversely, who believes that all of the generosity and consideration can or should run in only one direction? The answer to that is clearly not someone who understands balance or harmony, but rather, is someone who has become stuck in the slavelike labor of accumulating symbols of self-worth.

As we stockpile the prizes, the bonuses, and the fruits of advantage, if we have made the mistake of equating character with what we have collected, then we will fear its removal. Hence we will feel compelled to keep adding more and more to the portfolio of things that we believe define us. There shouldn't be a target point we feel we have to reach before we get around to giving back. We shouldn't do it just because we reached a comfort level with our money and our reputations. Service is not a social plum to be pulled out of the pie of success. We don't polish our medals with it. We find our humanity with it.

Gut Check

The dusty blue sedan with the one missing hubcap pulls into a metered parking spot that is ordinarily unavailable, even after all the stores along the boulevard have closed. But tonight is Christmas Eve, and the restaurants that usually swallow up the evening parking are all closed. A young mother sorts through what she laughingly calls her "savings account"—the change bin that slides out from under the car radio—in search of a quarter. Her two children, a boy of seven and a girl of nine, clamber out of the back seat and onto the sidewalk without their typical bickering, because Mom has brought them on a mysterious mission and they don't know what to expect.

They walk up the block and enter a building that looks like a motel, though more brightly lit and full of 'maids' wearing nursing caps. Mom approaches a large island of a desk in the middle of the lobby nervously clutching a shopping bag that she has pulled from the trunk of the car, unsure of how to present herself. She explains that she had called earlier in the day, inquiring about whether there was anyone here at the nursing home who might welcome a visit, even from people they'd never heard of, on Christmas Eve.

The head nurse brightens as she recalls the conversation. It was unusual bordering on odd, someone calling in with a request like that. For so many of the visitors that she observed, arriving here was a chore to be administered rather than an experience to be appreciated. And she had just the resident in mind. Mrs. Taylor down the hall in 116 was lying in her bed in a room with a big snowflake taped to her mirror, listening to Andy Williams quietly singing Christmas songs on a small tape player. Mrs. Taylor's relatives all lived far away, and if they came at all, it was during their summer vacations; she'd been expecting no one on this night, and she was willing to welcome some strangers in her room.

As the nurse leads the trio down the hall, brother and sister cringe at the sight and sound of an old man moaning loudly from his stationary wheelchair. The nurse pats his knee and tells him she'll be right back to rearrange him. Mom wonders if she's made a mistake, bringing her unsuspecting children to a place so full of frailty and physical failure on a night that should be jolly and bright. She looks at her offspring, walking gingerly past room after room, peeking into the doorways with wide eyes and tight lips. They can't turn back now.

The nurse announces their presence to Mrs. Taylor, who reaches down to smooth the wrinkles off her blanket. The nurse leaves quickly to tend to the elderly man in the hall, and the Christmas celebrants all take quiet stock of each other before Mom introduces the kids. Mrs. Taylor compliments them on their nice appearance and offers a plastic cup of apple juice, the only libation in the room. The children politely accept, and Mom moves quickly to perform the serving task for Mrs. Taylor. When she has finished filling the cups, she quickly pulls up her shopping bag for the elderly woman to see. "I don't know if you like decorations," she says almost apologetically, "but we have a few that there just wasn't any more room for at our house."

She removes a wood-and-velvet angel and hands it to Mrs. Taylor, who nearly gasps in surprise. "It's beautiful," she says. "Can you put it on the dresser so that everyone can see it?" A brass star and a small tapestry featuring a reindeer come out of the bag to Mrs. Taylor's continued delight, and she delights in placing them around her small room, so that whichever direction she may turn her head, there will be a visible reminder of the holiday season. Last to come out of Mom's shopping bag is a pewter candlestick with a crimson candle in it, and this Mrs. Taylor places on the table next to her bed, saying "I'm not supposed to have candles burning in here, but—oh, what the heck. I'll blow it out when you leave."

With the candle flickering gamely in the room's ventilation, the group gathers in close around Mrs. Taylor. Sipping apple juice and smiling brightly, she regales them with stories of other Christmases in places far different from this. She gets the children laughing when she tells them about her deceased husband's attempts to put up the annual Christmas tree, one that he always insisted on cutting down himself after paying the forest service a fee and driving fifty miles into the wilderness. The children tell her about the shopping mall Santa they recently encountered, with the crooked beard and the beeper that kept going off. They share memories that they don't have in common, a temporary family reuniting around a candle instead of a roaring fire, but the spirit lives in this room tonight. Mom may be unsure about a lot of things in her life, but she knows that something right is happening as the hectic season merges with the small event in room 116. She gives Mrs. Taylor a small box of chocolates, and the senior woman reciprocates by hunting in her purse for a pair of dollar bills, which she tucks gently into the children's hands.

Another silence settles over them, but this one is not at all awkward. Mrs. Taylor reaches out, and the four of them hold hands until it seems the elderly woman's arms are just beginning to wilt. They wish each other a Merry Christmas, and Mom leads the kids toward the door. "Do you want me to blow out the candle?" she stops to ask. Mrs. Taylor gazes at the candle flame, which has burned a long way down the stick. Then she smiles and shakes her head and shoos them cheerfully out the door, past the nurse, who whispers to them as they pass by, "Don't you worry. That candle can burn for a little while longer tonight."

Edwards strongly emphasizes the importance not only of realizing that every waking moment is a privilege, but also of acting on that realization. He says, "I incorporate this life principle into everything. God knows I'm not perfect—He and I discuss that fact quite often—but there is an uplifting quality in the honest attempt to serve a higher purpose, or at least a purpose that doesn't put us at the center of the universe. I am very fortunate to have that built right into my job with the Jets, and I never look back at a draft, a practice, a game, or a season without feeling grateful for the opportunity."

While the Jets have met with success on the field, the coach knows that he holds but just a share in it; he knows that he is not the sole cause. He doesn't suit up, bang helmets, turn his ankle, or count the bone bruises. As much as the execution of a game plan is concerned, he is only a part of it. What Herm does do is to trust the coaches and the players, because they are the ones who have to go out and transform ideas and concepts into the physical reality of a winning effort. He leads them down the right road, and that they're willing to follow. You take a head coach and everything that he represents—his experience, his instincts about the game and about people, his level of analysis, his imagination—and what you distill out of all that is someone who can provide some direction. That's what the head coach is supposed to do. You give others some direction and if it's the right direction and you've managed to earn their trust, it can be a worthwhile unified effort.

Anyone in a position of holding the trust of others should be humbled by the exchange. You can lead by other means, but if you're doing it by virtue of the trust you've earned, then it marks your character rather than your ability to be coercive or intimidating. And if that kind of connection is strong, and true, then you're standing as a person with integrity. Edwards says, "When I'm standing before the team, it's not as the definition of a football coach but as a man. And when I think of the responsibility of being in that position, with people I respect so much, it is always humbling. That energizes me. That gives me direction. That shores up my faith that if I keep leading the way I'm supposed to, the team will keep believing, the coaches will coach the way they're supposed to, the team will keep executing, and we'll find success together."

Edwards remains balanced by allowing the forward vision, the attitude with the goals and intentions that lie ahead, to be supported by the power of what has come before. He is able to access the pride or satisfaction of his own accomplishments as a starting point, as a means of getting his feet planted in the present, but there is so much more strength and inspiration available when he reflects on all that has preceded him in this game of football and the game of life. He makes this an exercise, one just as important as the physical conditioning that he continues to perform, because like all of us, he knows he could easily begin to take this opportunity for granted, or become falsely convinced that this is strictly the result of his own efforts.

Edwards reflects often on all the great opportunities he has been given. That's how achievement comes to us in this life. And if we're honest enough and diligent enough in our pursuit of self-awareness, we'll recognize that. We act on our own with borrowed or inherited tools. It is the rare person indeed who achieves anything in this life with absolute autonomy. Someone or something has provided the opportunity to move forward—parents, genes, a teacher, a cop, a scholarship fund, a coach who saw something, a sibling who listened, a partner who shared failure, a friend who said "yes"—and off we go, ready to make our contribution to the world.

There is a pleasant paradox that exists between the idea that we are all unique and the idea that there is nothing entirely new under the sun. The former idea recognizes that there will be distinction in what we do because we are who we are and the circumstances for every opportunity are going to be different somehow; there will be variation in the tools available and the challenge presented. The latter idea recognizes that mankind has been collectively yearning for the same things for a long, long time, and that if we assume to be the "be all" and "end all" in anything we do, then we are guilty of disrespecting the remarkable efforts that preceded us, and also (hopefully) even more efforts that will follow us. We want to stand at the midpoint of those ideas, looking ahead at the stamp we want to put on our time in the game, and reaching behind us for the tools that will enable us to do that.

"What did I do to make the game better?" Herm knows what others did; their accomplishments were like food, nourishment for his love and respect for the game. Edwards is aware that at this point in his life and career, he is being observed in some of the same ways by those who inspired him, so it is very important to keep his attitude "in shape." It is vital to remember all the contributions that brought readiness to him reflecting on all the things that have been done for him, large and small. He says, "If I believe that if I can give back half of what I have been fortunate enough to receive, then I'm heading in the right direction."

Gut Check

The appeals started coming in the spring. The young lawyer was fascinated with cause and effect as an occupational interest, and so he tried to connect the mailing list with the purchase he had made, or the event he had attended. Most of this sort of mailbox stuffing ended up in the recycling bin, but he thought it more sporting to throw it out, having first figured out its angle. Sometimes he deliberately misspelled his name to see how far and wide his identity was flung. It wasn't exactly cynicism on his part, but he found a strange amusement in analyzing his own exploitation as a potential customer or donor.

One day he held in his hand a mailer from Habitat for Humanity and wondered how they had found this private audience with him. He sat at the dining room table going through his mail while his pregnant wife watched her favorite TV show on the big screen in the living room and flashed on his purchase of the new German-made 4-horsepower miter saw awaiting its first use in the garage. Maybe there was a connection there. Or perhaps the loyalty he was showing to his news magazine subscription translated into the profile of a social activist on one mailing list or another. Did the vacation that he and his wife took to the Mexican Caribbean on a major credit card suggest a sensitivity to the third world that an alert charity could jump on? It made for interesting speculation.

One thing was sure: they were persistent. Every couple of weeks a new mailing came in, and every couple of weeks it found its way into the green bin along with the aluminum cans and the brown shopping bags. But something about this brochure spoke to him in a way that most of the others did not. With this humanitarian project, donors lent not only money but also time and sweat, helping people build houses that they would otherwise not be able to afford. The lawyer had grown up in a well to do, secluded social environment, where the sense of community was something to be purchased along with club memberships. The Habitat mailers described encounters between people in which demographics were irrelevant, where everyone was working with equal effort and value toward a common goal. It made satisfying sense to the young lawyer.

So eventually he overcame his tendency to layback and leave the heavy lifting to more outgoing people. He examined what was good in his own life and decided that there was something missing. He could no longer justify spending all his free time searching for the right piece of furniture, playing golf, or getting to all the social events that his group of friends seemed to be constantly generating.

One Saturday morning, he showed up at a housing site an hour's drive from home and modestly presented himself to the project coordinator, a shiny hammer dangling from an unscarred tool belt. He was sent off with a college freshman and a claims adjuster to frame in some bedroom walls. By the end of the day, his hammer was dulled by an equal number of scrapes and bull's eyes, and his belt looked like something that could now hang proudly on a hook. The thumb and forefinger on his nail-setting hand were a little on the purple side, but pride in a rare accomplishment proved to be an effective anesthetic. He had made a couple of great friends. And he was building a house for some people who otherwise wouldn't have one.

He kept coming back, hungry to learn, eager to contribute. One day, the fancy German miter saw came with him. He'd never actually used it. But one of his more experienced friends showed him the basics and he got to work. That day, he only stopped for ten minutes to eat his ham sandwich. There were too many tricky cuts to make on the window trim.

We all have people we respect, who inspire us, people whom we look up to. These are people who plainly possess characteristics we wish were stronger in us. We may wish we had the native ability to throw a football on target seventy-five yards in the air, or to win the yellow jersey for a segment of the Tour de France. That's elite territory, and it's frankly not available to everybody. We have our heroes, though, and they perform in those arenas on our behalf. Oftentimes, that's a satisfying experience, as we participate vicariously in the defeat of obstacles that have largely imaginary meaning in our own lives. Sometimes, it's not so satisfying; our heroes are not all capable of supplying an element of character to the physical achievement, and we know instinctively when we've had to compromise our own character in order to join the fan club.

But there are people who are capable of tapping into the spirit to deepen their physical gifts, and there is a magnetic attraction to them. Why? Because breaking the tape or kicking the game-winning field goal is not enough for these folks. Because service without the expectation or demand of something in return is unbelievably attractive and empowering. These are the givers. These are the heroes, squared.

Fine, we say. But doesn't a coach, or a parent, or a teacher demand performance in return for his or her investment in time and energy? Isn't that an understood part of the deal? A good teacher may require this quid pro quo. A teacher may deliver the goods and expect that there will be some return on his or her investment in time and energy. But a great teacher won't. A great teacher is a catalyst for some kind of journey of self-discovery, as much for himself as for the people he's guiding. A great teacher will stimulate a hunger for the possibilities rather than obedience to a strict technique. A great teacher knows instinctively that the measure is not taken in the stats accumulated by his students. He doesn't bask in reflected glory. There is a destiny of his own to fulfill.

In growing and learning, Herm paid close attention to the lessons learned from "the broom." He wanted to be successful and well respected in the game he so loved. Since he was able to play three times longer than the average pro, he achieved a certain degree of vocational and financial security. And although his schedule is now quite busy, he is never too busy, when he returns to that same small house, to yank the broom off its hook in the garage. Some small chore like that could easily be delegated and paid for. But not Herman.

This is his mother's house, after all, and he knows that her life would be just a little bit easier if she didn't have to chase the dirt out of the corners of her backyard haven. So any time Herm is in town he drops by to "take care of business," to push and pull the broom with speed and precision and build the pile of leaves and twigs and dust until it is ready for bagging. Martha often stands in the kitchen listening to the reassuring shreesh of broom bristles on concrete. The " shreeshing" is done with no fanfare or extra attention brought to the task—it is done because it's the right thing to do. The son is never foolish enough to think that this small favor begins to repay the mother for all the things she has done for him. But he is wise enough to know that the account would never be settled within himself if he didn't.

The Official's Call

Since I was twelve, I wanted to be a coach. I spent the six years in secondary school and four years in college observing my teachers and coaches. Every one of them, good, bad, right, or wrong became a mentor. I quickly discarded methods or techniques that I felt wouldn't serve a purpose for me. Yes, you can learn even from poor examples as well as from good ones.

Both my father and mother helped shape the values and principles that I hold dear today. A few years back, I wrote a book called Impartial Judgment and dedicated it to my father who "taught me to believe in myself." His lessons on discipline, commitment, and truthfulness served me well as a teacher, coach, high school principal, superintendent, and NFL referee. It is these same principles that I speak about today with corporate America. The opportunity to teach these ideas and ideals to CEOs is not much different from those young people with whom I have worked.

Through my years of teaching, I also learned that service to others was an idea to which I became attached. Zig Ziglar, the outstanding motivational speaker, told me a long time ago, "You can get everything you want in life, if you just help others get what they want." I believe in that mantra, and my efforts to help Herman in his "mission" has proven that.

I felt that as an NFL referee, my role was to "serve the game of football." I asked myself the same question you've heard Herman ask his players, "Did I make the game better today?" Too often, fans look at the officials as the "enemy"—"they're on the field to call fouls only on my team." Certainly, calling fouls is an important aspect of an official, but his greater purpose is to serve the players, coaches, and fans by properly conducting all phases of the game.

I remember phoning my mom several years back, she was eighty-nine at that time, and during our conversation she said, "Wait a minute, I have another call." When she returned to my line, I said, "Mom, do you have two phone lines in your home?"

I continued, "I grew up in that house; I don't remember having two phone lines." In fact, we only had one phone (instrument) in the entire house. She said, "No, I don't have two phones, I have 'call waiting.'"

I said, "Call waiting? Mom, you're eighty-nine, why do you need call waiting? Who was that on the other line?"

"Oh," she said, "the Carmelites are having a fund-raising luncheon next Tuesday, and I'm taking the reservations. That was Maxine saying she would be there."

I responded saying, "Mom at eighty-nine you are taking the reservations? Don't they have anyone forty-five or so that can do this?"

She said, "Well, no one volunteered at our last meeting, so I said I would do it."

Wow! Mom continued to "step up" to help others. I look forward to continuing that legacy.

CHAPTER 9

Diversity and the Intern Program

The National Football League, in 1987, started an "intern program" called the Minority Coaching Fellowship Program. For Edwards, it came about at the right time in his career. He is a head coach in the NFL today and extremely grateful of the opportunity the program provided. The intern program offers summer training camp internships to minority coaches who want to develop their skills, as well as to add something to their football knowledge.

After finishing his college playing days at San Diego State, in 1977, Edwards was not sure what he wanted to do. He had dreamed—and occasionally bragged—about playing in the NFL but wasn't drafted. The NFL had 12 rounds and drafted 335 players. Edwards wasn't one of them. And of course, that bothered him. His degree in business administration from San Diego State had prepared him for the world of work, which was a viable choice.

Then two calls came. The first was from Carl Peterson, general manager of the Philadelphia Eagles and the other from Don Shula, head coach of the Miami Dolphins. Coach Shula wanted Herm to come immediately (July 1977) to the Dolphins' training camp, which he did. Coach Shula liked what he saw in Edwards's abilities and wanted to sign him right then and there at that camp. Edwards had already promised Carl Peterson that he would give the Eagles a "look." There was no question he would keep that promise. And he did. Herm reported to the Eagles training camp, signed and played ten years in the NFL.

When Edwards was about in his ninth year, the Eagles decided it was time for him to go (read: release him). But Herm still wanted to play. Accepting a trade to the Los Angeles Rams, who later released him, he then moved on to the Atlanta Falcons. But, after the 1987 season, it was time for him to leave the playing field—an athlete "just knows" when that time has come. Returning home to the Monterey Peninsula (California) not sure how to get his life and career going, he turned to friends around town. One was Jim Cota, who was his Pony League Coach and had a successful moving and storage business. Jim offered Herm a job, and he was eager to get started. That day was a Friday. On Saturday, Carl Peterson—yes, the same Carl Peterson—called. Only now, he was the president/ general manager/ chief operating officer of the Kansas City Chiefs. He told Herm about the intern program and asked him to join the Chiefs and Head Coach Marty Schottenheimer in a scouting and coaching position. Herm accepted and with a quick phone call to Mr. Cota—leaving a message on his answering machine—on Saturday, was on a plane out of Monterey to Kansas City. It was the right move at the right time.

At Kansas City, his job was scouting college players and working with the defensive secondary. It was here he became reacquainted with Tony Dungy, who was the defensive secondary coach. Tony and Herm knew each other when Tony played for the Minnesota Vikings and Herm was with the Eagles. Their relationship at the Chiefs grew to a strong personal as well as professional friendship. There they developed a healthy respect for each other's talents.

With the Chiefs, Edwards scouted both pro and college players, and when Dungy left Kansas City to be the defensive coordinator at Minnesota; Herm became the Chiefs' defensive secondary coach.

When Tony Dungy was offered the head coaching job with the Tampa Bay Bucs in 1996, he asked Herm to join him there as defensive backfield coach. It was a dilemma. At the Chiefs, Herm was progressing well, and Carl Peterson was an excellent mentor. Herm didn't want to offend him by leaving to go to the Bucs, but Carl's position was clear. "Herman," he said, "there's a strong future for you in the NFL coaching ranks. Take it and go with Tony." Carl's thinking was always in Herman's best interests. He joined Tony at Tampa Bay in 1996.

While at Kansas City, Herm had also worked with Terry Bradway, who was the Chiefs' director of player personnel. Peterson, always the mentor, was helping develop Bradway into general-manager material. Peterson succeeded, and so did Bradway. Terry told Herm that if and when he became a general manager, he'd be first on his list to call as head coach. Wow, Edwards's dream was developing as he hoped it would.

Then, it happened. On Tuesday, January 9, 2001, Terry was at the East-West Game in San Francisco watching the college all-stars practice. He got a call from the Jets requesting he come to New York to interview for the general manager's job. Terry tells it this way: "I left San Francisco and had to go to Kansas City to pick up some clothes, then fly to New York for my interview. In the SFO Airport I called Herm to break the good news, and I said, 'Herm, I am being interviewed for the general manager job at the Jets. Would you be interested in becoming the head coach?"

Terry continues, "And you know what Herm said to me on the phone? 'Go get the job!' Can you imagine, here I am offering Herm an opportunity to be an NFL head coach and all he thinks about is me—'Go get the job.'" Terry flew to New York and did get the job. The Jets had been in turmoil and needed some stability. Bill Parcells had resigned as general manager. They were also looking for their third head coach in three years.

Sunday, January 14, Terry's first interview for the head coach was Maurice Carthon, a great running back from the New York Giants, who was then an assistant coach with the Jets. Later that same day, Terry called Herm and asked him to come for an interview. Arriving in New York he met with Terry and Mike Tannenbaum who was the Jets' assistant general manager-director of pro personnel.

You couldn't call that dinner/meeting "fast food." They talked for five hours. The next day Herm met with Terry and the owner, Mr. Robert (Woody) Johnson IV, the heir to the Johnson & Johnson Pharmaceutical Company who had recently bought the Jets for $700 million.

The interview lasted seven hours! And Johnson was there the whole time. He was involved from the beginning. He is still "involved" as the owner of the Jets, however, he allows Terry, the staff, and Coach Edwards to run the show. He's the kind of owner Herm always hoped to work for. In all fairness though, that accolade must include Mr. Lamar Hunt, owner of the Kansas City Chiefs since

1960, as an owner who has all the qualities a coach wants.

The Jets had also interviewed Dom Capers, who had been head coach at the Jacksonville Jaguars but was fired after the 1999 season. Then they interviewed Ted Cottrell who was the Buffalo Bills defensive coordinator. Cottrell was a formidable head-coaching candidate. In his seven seasons with the Bills he had developed them into becoming a top-rated defense respected by every opponent they faced.

After his interview, Herm went to Mobile, Alabama, to scout college players practicing for the Senior Bowl. Terry called him in Mobile and said, "Herm, come on back to New York; you're going to be our head coach." And on January 18, 2001, Herman Edwards was named head coach of the New York Jets and met the curious New York press for the first time. The next press conference was in, of all places, Tampa, Florida on Saturday, January 27, where Super Bowl XXXV was to be played the next day between the New York Giants and the Baltimore Ravens. It was quite a press conference, with all the New York Press in town for the Giants game. So, naturally, they all came, about a hundred-plus reporters, to that press conference.

And so it began—"Mr. Bob" from the little coastal town of Seaside, California, who shined U.S. Army soldiers shoes at Fort Ord for thirty-five cents now was standing in front of a hundred-plus New York reporters and TV cameras in Tampa, Florida, answering questions about how he was going to lead the New York Jets "to victory."

Edwards says, "I am proud to be the first candidate, who was given the opportunity in the NFL Intern Program, to become a head coach. I also know that along with that opportunity is a responsibility. The responsibility to not only make my family and my team proud of what I do, but also to uphold the position and task given to me. I know others will follow in my footsteps, and many others will be hoping to do so also. My job is to do the best job I can; 'Get the corners,' as my father would say and, 'Son, don't be afraid of the broom.' 'Thanks, Dad, I'm not.'"

When the opportunity to interview for an NFL head-coaching job would come—and he knew someday it would—Herm wanted to be prepared. In 1999, as the assistant head coach (to Tony Dungy) and defensive coordinator of the Bucs, Marty Schottenheimer, head coach of the Kansas City Chiefs, resigned; Herm was at the Senior Bowl in Mobile and called Carl Peterson, the Chiefs' president. Herm said, "Carl, I know I don't have a chance to get that job, but would you interview me?" He was just wanting to have the experience of a head coach's job interview. Carl was gracious enough to conduct a formal interview, and Herm was ready. He went into the interview with not only a resume but also a plan of action on how—as head coach—he could make the Chiefs a winner. Even knowing that Carl would not offer him the job, his plan and thinking was to "go into that interview ready to accept an offer." Some two hours later that day Herm called Carl and said, "Well, how'd I do? Tell me my strengths and the areas I need to improve on to do a better job." He did, and made the necessary adjustments for a better presentation.

Let's be clear about diversity. Diversity is absolutely no replacement for excellence, ability, and individual hard work. Too often, it seems we get "rights" mixed up with opportunity. When an opportunity comes, we have the right to work hard to use that opportunity to further ourselves. Success with that opportunity ought to be the results of your labor. The opportunity—and the job itself—is a privilege, not a right.

In the spring of 2003, Edwards was asked to speak about the intern program to the NFL owners meeting in Palm Springs. Speaking from his beliefs and experiences, he laid it out this way, "Anyone, minority or not, who has an opportunity to interview for a job should do the interview. Whether you think the job is already spoken for or not, it doesn't matter. Take the opportunity to learn from it. You will only be better next time."

The 2007 season is Edwards's twenty-eighth year in the NFL— seventh as Head Coach. Does he consider himself "fortunate?" Of course. Many others with that number of years—or more—have not made it to this position. If you look at Edwards's beginnings, you might draw the conclusion that he came from a "less fortunate background." He never, ever considered that. He always believes that if you work hard and do the right thing, good things will happen to you.

Opportunities are now emerging more than ever in the history of the NFL. Minority candidates are now coming forth from all areas— the front offices, coaching ranks, NFL Minority Coaching Fellowship Program, NFL Europe League, and even from those who are in the Pro Football Hall of Fame.

The Baltimore Ravens promoted Pro-Football Hall of Famer Ozzie Newsome from senior vice-president to general manager and executive vice-president. Newsome, also a member of the NFL Competition Committee, was responsible for bringing to the Ravens many of the players who helped the team win its Super Bowl XXXV title. Eleven of the starters in that game were Ravens draft choices. The naming of Newsome to this role was followed by a succession of similar appointments of African-Americans to high-ranking positions in college and in the NFL.

Key appointments during 2003 were Marvin Lewis, head coach of Cincinnati Bengals. The second graduate from the NFL Minority Coaching Fellowship Program was also in the program at Kansas City in 1991 with Carl Peterson and Marty Schottenheimer. Rod Graves, vice president of Football Operations for Arizona Cardinals was named by Cardinals owner Bill Bidwill to that newly created position. The forty-three-year old Graves is a nineteen-year veteran of scouting and was with Carl Peterson and Terry Bradway as director of College Scouting in the USFL and served in other player personnel positions with the Chicago Bears and Cardinals. He is also a member of the NFL Management Council's Working Group Committee and the NFL College Advisory Committee.

James Harris, vice president of player personnel for Jacksonville Jaguars, was one of the first black quarterbacks to start in the NFL. Harris enjoyed a twelve-year playing career with the Buffalo Bills, the Los Angeles Rams, and the San Diego Chargers before moving into scouting/personnel roles with the New York Jets, Tampa Bay Bucs, and most recently, Baltimore. Harris and Edwards were together on Dungy's staff.

Karl Dorrell, Head Coach at UCLA, is another graduate of the NFL Minority Coaching Program (Denver Broncos, 1993 and 1999). The thirty-nine-year old Dorrell comes to one of the most visible Division-I college programs after three years as the Denver Bronco's wide receivers coach.

Also during the spring of 2003, six African-American coaches were newly appointed to coordinator roles, one step below the head coaching position. Hue Jackson, former offense from the Washington Redskins, was a 1995 participant in the NFL Minority Coaching Fellowship with the Redskins. He also received coaching experience from NFL Europe with London in 1991. Leslie Frazier is the defensive coordinator of the Cincinnati Bengals, hired by head coach Marvin Lewis. Maurice Carthon, offense from Dallas Cowboys. This former NFL running back rejoined Cowboys coach Bill Parcells, for whom he played with the New York Giants, and coached with Parcells at the New England Patriots and New York Jets. George Edwards, defense from Washington Redskins, was promoted to coordinator after one season with Washington following four years as the linebackers' coach in Dallas. Sherman Lewis, former offensive coordinator of Green Bay and Minnesota, assumed the same role with Detroit. Ray Rhodes, defense from Seattle Seahawks, was a former head coach of the Philadelphia Eagles and the Green Bay Packers; he joined the Seahawks after two seasons as Denver's defensive coordinator.

In 2003, there was a record of fourteen African-American coordinators in the NFL. The latest appointments join those already in place: Greg Blache, defense, Chicago; Romeo Crennel, defense, New England; Ted Cottrell, defense, New York Jets; Jerry Gray, defense, Buffalo; Tim Lewis, defense, Pittsburgh; Johnnie Lynn, defense, New York Giants; and Ron Meeks, defense, Indianapolis. Other appointments have been made since this writing.

In 2004, Lovie Smith was selected as the head coach of the Chicago Bears. The Baltimore Ravens appointed pro-football Hall of Famer, Mike Singletary as their linebackers coach. The leader of the Chicago Bears' famed "forty-six defense" who helped the Bears win Super Bowl XX, assumed his first NFL coaching role. "I'm not trying to coach; I'm going to coach," says Singletary. "Anything that I'm going to do, I will do with all my heart and all my mind and all my soul. This is where I'm supposed to be." Mike knows about the word "try"—he knows that it only gives a person an excuse for failure. Mike Singletary joined Willie Brown (Oakland), Joe Greene (Arizona), Charlie Joiner (Kansas City), and James Lofton (San Diego) as other Hall of Famers who are current NFL assistant coaches.

The Official's Call

My wife, Linda, and I were in the audience sitting next to Lia (Mrs. Edwards) at that press conference in Tampa. I had known Herm for about twenty years at that point and was somewhat apprehensive about him facing an aggressive group of New York reporters. Herman is such a straight-on guy that he never "blinked" once at their penetrating questions. He is honest in his answers and handled each question the same way he handled "the broom." He reached into the "corners" and attended to the details expertly. He never let them steal his grin. Herman Sr. would have been proud to be there—and maybe he was!

Diversity never seemed to be an issue in the NFL officiating ranks. When I was hired in 1960, eight other officials were also added to the corps. Prior to 1960 there were only twelve teams in the NFL, with crews of five, so the total number of officials at that time was about thirty. There were six games each Sunday (no Monday nights then), with five in each officiating crew.

The reason for adding nine officials in 1960 was that the Dallas Cowboys were joining the existing twelve NFL teams with the Minnesota Vikings scheduled to join in 1961. No African-American officials were on the staff nor were among the nine of us hired in 1960. It is interesting to note, however, that in 1954, the NFL-hired Joe Gonzales, of Hispanic heritage. Joe had been a successful, and well respected, high school and college official. He had a successful twenty-year officiating career in the NFL and was well accepted by officials, coaches, and players.

In the same year, 1960, the American Football League (AFL) was formed to provide more opportunities for players and coaches, as well as for officials. The AFL was just beginning their league and had to build an officiating corp of about thirty-three officials. The AFL was totally separate—commissioner, league headquarters, teams, and officials—from the NFL. I was also invited to become an AFL official in 1960, but I chose the longer-standing, well-established NFL. As history shows, the two leagues "warred" until they agreed to merge in 1968. The AFL chose Aaron Wade, an African-American high school and college official in 1965. What helped Aaron move to the professional level was his successful high-school coaching career. Aaron was head football coach at Centennial High School in Compton, California, and had produced several players who went on to become NFL stars. While Aaron may not have had the necessary college experience that his colleagues had, he certainly had knowledge of the game through his former players.

In 1965, the NFL hired its first African-American official: Burl Toler from San Francisco. Although Burl had limited college officiating experience; he brought a strong football background to the NFL. Burl was captain of a University of San Francisco football team that sent nine players—from one team—to the NFL. Among them were Ollie Matson, Gino Marchetti, and Bob St. Clair. Each had a long and distinguished NFL career. Burl, himself, was selected out of college to play in the all-star game in Chicago in 1951. The all-star game had the best college players playing the NFL Champions—Los Angeles Rams—in a preseason game. Although drafted by the Cleveland Browns, Burl never got to play in the NFL. He broke his leg in that all-star game, which ended his playing career.

Burl was a junior high teacher and principal in San Francisco. His personality was always that of a teacher—smiling, laughing, and pleasant to be around. He had a couple of friends from San Francisco already in the league, Armen Terzian and Grover Klemmer, who helped make his transition into the NFL an easy one. Burl was assigned to a crew headed by Norm Schachter, a proven referee and leader. Norm, later the referee in Super Bowl I (1967), was an excellent teacher and mentor for many young officials. Burl loved working with Norm and adjusted well to officiating.

I was able to get to know Burl, his late wife, Mel, and all six of their children, because I was fortunate enough to work with Burl in our crew for eleven seasons. You get to know a guy pretty well when you are together for eleven years, some twenty weekends each year. We remain good friends. Burl worked twenty-five years as an NFL head linesman including playoff games and Super Bowl XIV. In 1968, the NFL added a second African-American to its group. Bob Beeks, a police officer in his day-in-and-day-out job, had gained his officiating experience in the St. Louis area.

In NFL officiating, there is no apparent distinction regarding ethnic background. The more important issue is successful experience on the field. That's the true and only criteria the league should—and I believe—has employed. There are now twenty-four African-American officials in the NFL who have earned that right through successful experiences in the major colleges, in NFL Europe, and in the arena leagues.

A young African-American official named Johnny Grier was among those hired in 1981. As a referee, I always enjoyed "rookies" being assigned to our crew. I believe it helps veterans from becoming complacent and involves them as teachers of younger officials. Johnny was assigned the position of field judge (now called back judge) on our crew and worked with the late Pat Knight and the late

Gil Mace, two veteran officials on the defensive side of the ball. As the referee and crew chief, I enjoyed being part of Johnny's first four years. Johnny was assigned to the position of referee in 1988, the first black to be named to that position. Johnny concluded his twenty-third year in 2003 in that position and is one of the seventeen who work in the position of referee, along with Mike Carey, also an African-American.

Of the twenty-four African-American Officials on its staff of 119, some also serve on the board of the National Football League Referees Association (NFLRA), a union that was formed in 1993. The director of officiating (league office staff), Larry Upson, is also African-American. Others serve as supervisor and observers/scouts for the league.

Balance, equal opportunity, and fairness are criteria the league strives to uphold. And it does.

CHAPTER 10

Practicing in January

"You want to be practicing in January," Coach Edwards told the Jets players and coaches on Christmas Eve 2003. "That's when good things are happening—the playoffs. However, we are not going to the playoffs this year. There may be seasons like this, but we'll get through them."

The 2003 season for the Jets looked very promising. In 2001, Jets made the playoffs. In 2002, it was even better because they won the AFC East Division Championship. Coach Edwards and the team looked forward to a great 2003 season.

Even the loss of five key players—Coles, Morton, Turk, Hall, and Anderson (see chapter 11)—did not dampen their enthusiasm. Curtis Conway was acquired to "step up" at the receivers spot. The Jets repositioned their 2003 draft picks in April 2003 to acquire Rookie Dewayne Robinson to strengthen a defensive line that gave up too many yards per game in 2002. Their opponents used that weakened line to pound out a running game that placed the Jets 29 (out of thirty-two) in yielding defensive yards rushing.

However, John Abraham, Shaun Ellis, Aaron Beasley, Sam Cowart, and Mo Lewis were a strong nucleus to rebuild that 2002 defense. The offense under the emerging leadership and passion of quarterback Chad Pennington had gained respect not only in the AFC East but posed a threat to every Jet opponent through the NFL. WR Santana Moss was expected to use his lightning speed and ability to "get open" and be the "go to guy" as a receiver. The punt and kickoff return teams offered the same potential threat in 2003 as it did in 2002 with Moss every time he touched the ball.

The NFL kickoff of the 2003 preseason, in its strategy to market its product worldwide, scheduled a game in Tokyo, Japan, in August. (I had the privilege of refereeing the first game ever played in Tokyo in 1976 [San Diego versus San Francisco], and a second in my last season, August 1990 [Denver and Seattle]).

The Jets were selected to play in Tokyo (now called the American Game Bowl) on August 2, 2003. It looked to be an interesting start of the season, with an opportunity to be the first New York team to play in that game. The Jets were anxious to go—even though their opponents would be the Tampa Bay Bucs, Super Bowl XXXVII champions! Wow, what a way to start the preseason.

Coach Edwards was looking forward to playing against his former team. Having been an assistant coach at Tampa Bay (under Head Coach Tony Dungy) he knew almost every player and the front office personnel of the Bucs. He didn't know, however, the Bucs head coach, Jon Gruden, very well. The Bucs won 30-14. Coach Gruden decided to sustain "championship" fever by playing his first team much longer in that (Tokyo) game than what preseason games call for. Coach Edwards, although always wanting to win ("You play to win the game"), wanted every one of the eighty players who made the trip to have the experience of "playing in Tokyo."

In the second preseason game, the Jets played the Cincinnati Bengals, now coached by Marv Lewis in his first year as head coach. This preseason match-up pitted the first two "minority" fellowship program coaches against each other. Herm was the first, and Marv was the second African-American to go through the program (see chapter 9) and become head coach in the NFL. It was a historic game day on August 10, 2003, as the Jets won 28-13 (Note: The Bengals finished second in the AFC South with an 8-8 record in the 2003 season.)

The third preseason game brought the New Orleans Saints to the Meadowlands on August 16. The Saints, coached by Jim Haslett, a former Buffalo Bills linebacker, were making great strides and were expected to challenge the Bucs for the NFL South title. The Saints defeated the Jets 22-17 that summer evening in New Jersey. (Note: The Saints and the Bucs finished the 2003 season at 8-8 and 7-9 respectively with the Carolina Panthers winning the NFC South at 10-6).

The fourth preseason game found the Jets "away" playing the New York Giants—at the Meadowlands—yes, that's the Jets home field also but they share the Meadowlands with the Giants who were "at home" for this game. Coach Edwards said, "It felt strange being 'at home' but seated on the 'visitors bench.' (I have refereed that "pride of New York [Giants versus Jets] game" many times. It was always a "battle,") and this 2003 match-up turned out to be no exception. The "exception," however, turned out to be a "turning point" in the Jets season.

Third quarter: Jets have the ball, Quarterback Chad Pennington No. 10 back to pass; receivers covered; scrambles to his right; but not fast enough as a linebacker tackles him from behind. Down to the ground goes Pennington with the Giants player landing on top of him. It happens in every NFL game—"QB sacked"—referee blows his whistle, signals time out to stop the clock (standard procedure on QB sack), and all the players get up to go back to their respective huddles for the next play.

But Pennington doesn't get up! He is hurt! Probably just got the wind knocked out of him. Time out—injury! Dr. Elliott Perlman, Jets team doctor, hustles onto the field. Pennington's hurt. Coaches, players, and fans say, "Oh no," and then "oh yes!" Pennington has landed on his left hand (he throws with his right)—probably just a sprain. Wrong! All metatarsal bones in Pennington's left hand were broken. Testaverde replaces Pennington. And Jets go on to win 15-14.

In the final preseason game, their fifth, with Testaverde as quarterback, the Jets beat the Philadelphia Eagles 17-0 at the new Lincoln Financial Field in Philadelphia. (Note: Although the Eagles did have a slow start in the 2003 season, they won the NFC East with a 12-4 record). Jets preseason results in three wins and two losses. Testaverde replaced Pennington, who was not expected back until the October 26 game at Philadelphia.

The Jets regular season, often called by the NFL as "championship season" because every game points toward the championship game called the Super Bowl, was planned to be a spectacular opening for Gang Green. The NFL likes to "jump start" its regular season with a special game—Thursday night (September 4) prior to its opening weekend. ESPN would televise nationally with everybody watching—Jets versus Washington Redskins in their new Fed Ex Stadium. Four Jets from the 2002 season were now principal players on the Redskins (see chapter 11): Coles, Morton, Thomas, and Hall. It was a great match-up, but the Redskins won 16-13.

The second, third, and fourth games resulted in three more losses, making it a 0-4 start for the Jets. They had played against Miami, New England, and Dallas; two of these teams making the 2003 play-offs. Just what the Jets—or any NFL team—didn't want. The 2002 season had started that way—with a 1-4 record—something the Jets coaches and players worked to avoid for the 2003 season. At 0-4, the first week in October 2003 was the Jets' bye week. Not much fun having a week off when you're 0-4. Every player, every coach wants to be "on the field" that next week to get a "win." Then an unexpected event occurred that placed Coach Edwards in a special class.

On Wednesday, October 1, 2003, at 1:30 a.m. Jets' defensive end John Abraham, 6'4", 256 pounds, a five-year veteran, was arrested for driving under the influence (commonly called a "DUI"). As it turned out, John did not have an alcohol problem but made the mistake of driving after he had been drinking. His DUI made headlines in all the New York papers, obviously not the image that the New York Jets wanted.

Coach Edwards took an action that (1) he had never before faced and (2) many coaches would not take or have not taken. He suspended John Abraham for one game without pay! This was during the Jets bye week, and they were scheduled to play the visiting Buffalo Bills in their next game on October 12—without John Abraham, their all-pro defensive end. Coach Edwards said, "The behavior of our players both on and off the field reflects on this New York Jets team. This is a learning lesson for both John and our football club." Herm is often quoted, "Nothing good happens after midnight."

The Jets defeated the Bills at home 30-3, even with John Abraham on the bench. The Jets then traveled to Houston, beating the Texans 19-14. On their eighth week at Philadelphia, Pennington was back! Wow! Two wins in a row and on to Philadelphia who, now gathering midseason strength, won 24-17. The Jets had defeated the Eagles 17-9 in preseason by eight points, but now they lost by seven. Next, the Giants, in the Meadowlands, who won in overtime 31-28. It was a tough loss to their cross-town rivals by three having beaten them ten weeks earlier.

The Jets then traveled to the "black hole" of the Oakland Raiders who had just lost Rich Gannon and Marques Tuiasosopo, their first and second team quarterbacks to injuries. Nonetheless, the Raiders at home are traditionally fierce opponents enhanced by their enthusiastic—and some say—vitriolic fans. This November 9 game in 2003 was the Jets' fourth trip across country in the three seasons of Edwards's head-coaching career. Pennington, now finding his rhythm, rallied the Jets in the fourth quarter to tie the game, sending it into overtime (24-24). He then drove the Jets down deep into Raiders territory as Doug Brien kicked the winning field goal. The Jets won 27-24 and were now 3-6 ready to face the Colts in Indianapolis the next week.

The Jets 2003 season is somewhat typified by that Colts game on November 16. The Colts won 38-31 not much of a defensive battle for two coaches—Edwards and Dungy—who played defense in the NFL and built their reputations on being defensive masters. At their midfield handshake meeting after the game Herman said to Tony, "I think we set defense in the NFL back ten years." However, what typified that game were two plays—two plays!—that made a difference: (1) a goal-line stand by the Jets when linebacker Sam Cowart was unable to wrap up RB Edgren James at the one-yard line as James scored on fourth down, and (2) a fake field goal by "holder" Hunter Smith who ran around left end and Jets linebacker Aaron Beasley for another score. The Jets were in the game except for two plays! (Note: I heard Coach Vince Lombardi tell his team one time, "Gentlemen, today's game will be decided by four plays. Now," he said, "I don't know which plays those will be, so play every play like it's one of those four.")

The Jets rallied from a 10-6 deficit with just three minutes remaining and no time outs left drove ninety-four yards in eleven plays in 2:34, going ahead 13-10 to defeat the Jaguars in Jacksonville in week twelve. And now they moved from fourth to third place in the AFC East to give them a great energy boost.

The next week's December 1 Monday-night game was with the AFC South division favorites Tennessee Titans who finished the season 12-4 and made it to the AFC Division playoffs. It was an exciting quarterback match-up: Pennington versus McNair. Interestingly, the New York Jets played their first game in the AFL (yes AFL not AFC) in 1960 under the moniker "New York Titans." Today's Tennessee Titans were originally the Houston Oilers. Moving to Tennessee, the Oilers in 1999 changed their name to the Tennessee

Titans. The Jets won 24-17, giving Coach Edwards his first win as head coach on Monday night football.

Now at 5-7, the Jets traveled to Buffalo (they had beaten the Bills at home 30-3 without Pennington), striving to keep ahead of the Bills in their division and to have a chance in the AFC wildcard race. Losing 17-6, the Jets dropped to 5-8, disappointed but never discouraged. "Quit—not on my watch," Coach Edwards repeated as the Pittsburgh Steelers came to the Meadowlands and the Jets greeted them with a 6-0 defeat in the biggest snowstorm of the season. For the first time that season, Pennington went without throwing a touchdown pass.

The AFC East Division leader, the New England Patriots next came visiting, bringing with them an eleven-game winning steak and a 12-2 record. It could easily be said that the Patriots were on "a roll" and at this time of the season looked to have home-field advantage and a good chance to be the Super Bowl AFC representative. In the 2003 season, everything seemed to go right for the Patriots; they won close games, their quarterback stayed healthy and although they had a number of injuries, the replacements "stepped up" to play better than anticipated. The Jets on the other hand didn't have a great day yet only lost by five points 21-16. Quarterback Pennington found out what a "bad day" really means. He threw forty-three times with twenty-four completions and five—yes, five—interceptions. Those five "turnovers" cost the Jets a chance to stay viable in the race for a wild card spot. (Note: the Jets needed help of other AFC wild-card contenders to lose but that didn't happen either).

"Turnovers are like a bad penny," Coach Edwards often says, and the Jets ended the season with a –1 in turnovers (meaning that they "turned the ball over—fumbles, interceptions—one more time than their opponents turned the ball over to them. The conference-leading Patriots, however, ended the season with a +17 turnover rating. And went on to win Super Bowl XXXVIII. That turnover ratio is a compelling statistic in championship teams.

Steve Young, the Hall-of-famer-to-be and now an ESPN analyst said, "Herman Edwards is a master motivator." And many of those who have watched Edwards coach the Jets in his first three seasons (10-6 in 2001, 9-7 in 2002, and 6-10 in 2003) agree with Young's statement. Herman teaches the Jets players and coaches to "believe in themselves." However, Edwards follows that with "to make belief work, action is required." Many heard Coach Edwards, "miked up" for the Monday-night football game with the Titans, saying, "Make a play, make a play, make a play." That's the action that summarily follows belief in one's self and one's teammates.

The "action" that Coach Edwards had planned for, prepared for, and hoped for, didn't happen in 2003. For any season to be a championship one, several ingredients must take place. First, you win the close ones. You must always "believe" you can and will win those. You do not just "try" (see chapter 4) to win, but you will win—as the title of this book says, "It's the will, not the skill." Seven of the sixteen games were lost by close scores: 3 by 3 points; 1 by 5 points; 3 by seven points (one touchdown); twelve games were decided in the fourth quarter, two in overtime. Eleven wins instead of six would put the Jets in the playoffs. Injuries always play a part. The loss of quarterback Pennington for seven games was, of course, critical. No other team lost their starting quarterback for that many games except the Oakland Raiders—Super Bowl XXXVII runners-up in 2002 and out of the playoffs in 2003. In addition to Pennington, the Jets lost several (no sense in listing all those) key players for more than one game each. In fact, the Jets not only activated several players from their "practice squad"; they also picked up other "players off the streets"—meaning several who were working at jobs out of football and were called as late as Wednesday to "suit up" for a Sunday game. The Cincinnati Bengals, under first-year coach Marv Lewis, who were playing for the AFC North Division title on the last Sunday of the 2003 season, did not have an injured player until the eleventh week of the season. The Bengals had the No. 1 draft choice, Carson Palmer, sitting on the bench the entire season—not one play—because well-traveled quarterback Jon Kitna had a breakthrough season. That's what parody, draft choices, trades, and free agency mean to the teams that end up "practicing in January."

"We'll find a way to get through this," Coach Edwards says. Notice that he doesn't say—we will "try" to find a way but that we "will find a way." Further, he states that they will "get through" this. It's almost as if it's a "rite of passage." My NFL history reminds me that I watched George Halas (Bears), Vince Lombardi (Packers), Don Shula (Colts-Dolphins), Tom Landry (Cowboys), Chuck Noll (Stealers), Hank Stram (Chiefs), Bill Walsh (49ers)—all Hall of Fame coaches "go through" seasons like this. Coach Herman Edwards is of that class of coaches. As Thomas George, sportswriter for the New York Times once wrote about Coach Edwards: "His encore is worth anticipating."

CHAPTER 11

Basic Elements of a Great Team: Chemistry and Sportsmanship

As Sister Sara (in the movie Guys and Dolls) said to Sky Masterson, "Chemistry? What do you mean? How will you know?" And Sky responds, "Chemistry? Yeah, chemistry. I'll know."

Chemistry. We know it when we see it, right? Even if it's invisible, weightless, and takes up no space. Even if we had run away from a lab full of beakers and test tubes in high school, we still know when we're under its spell. We can all name examples of chemistry, both good and not so good. The 1972 Miami Dolphins, the only team to ever go undefeated for an entire season in the NFL—now there's an example of good chemistry. On paper, they weren't that much better than the rest of the league. It was the additional ingredient, something that can't always be easily defined, that put that team of Don Shula's in a category of its own. Or take Jerry Lewis and Dean Martin. You wouldn't look at such a mismatched pair of entertainers and immediately think of long, sold-out runs in Las Vegas. But they had it. Conversely, we've all seen all-star teams that are "loaded" with the best players but fail to perform to the level expected.

Many of us have been part of some scenario that owed its success—or its lack of success—to the merging of human energies that we identify as chemistry for the sake of simplification. It's shorthand for what is sometimes a complex relationship of other factors that either encourage or discourage productivity and success. It's the code word for what our instincts tell us about a given relationship or situation. Chemistry (and this must be considered the finest kind) is a key element in Herm's marriage to Lia, and it is a focal point of their relationship with son, Marcus. It is also a high priority in the success of the Jets.

To say that it is a "priority" suggests that chemistry is not something that we wait for, hoping it will fall from heaven. It is not made of serendipity. Chemistry is something that will naturally result from the good work done in the honest pursuit of goals. It's an atmosphere of possibility, with a strong emphasis on trust and responsibility. From the time that Mr. Woody Johnson, owner, and Terry Bradway, general manager hired Edwards as head coach of the New York Jets (January 2001), he has created a climate of good chemistry. This requires a commitment of honesty with each other, of trusting each other, and of nurturing the best contributions in each other. If that is done, along with taking personal responsibility for each of our assigned jobs, then that indefinable thing we call "chemistry" can stay indefinable—because we'll have plenty of it.

Edwards repeatedly emphasizes, "Being honest is, as my father taught me, doing the right thing. For example, if I feel that Paul [Hackett, the Jets' offensive coordinator] is not setting up a game plan that I believe we need to win, I must tell him so. I do it in a constructive way. I must be honest with myself, so then I must be honest with him. That approach leads us to an agreement on a specific game plan."

"I trust our coaches and our players because I know they are honest with themselves. I know that because I am with them every day—every practice, every workout, every game. I can look each one in the eye, and I can feel his intent is honest.

I know it, and they know that I know—that's trust." Nurturing is caring. Herm learned a long time ago that "people don't care how much you know, until they know how much you care." The Jets players don't care how much he knows until they know how much he cares for them. That is why Coach Edwards inscribed on the front of the Jets' playbook "It's the will, not the skill." It is important, however, that he shows that care through nurturing. He takes his personal time and energy to listen to each one's concerns and help them in any way he can.

The "broom" taught him that accountability. The responsibility of "sweeping the leaves" was his. And his dad held him accountable.

Chemistry is key in building the Jets into a winning team—this is the deal. You can "buy" players, but you can't buy chemistry. Free agency in the NFL has damaged the chemistry that coaches strive to build. Free agency affects fan loyalty. Fans are an important element in the chemistry of any team or organization.

Free agency started in 1993. Its purpose was to give a player the ability to change teams when that player felt it necessary. There is an irony in that. When a player signs a contract (with a given team), he usually signs for a number of years (average three or four years). He does so to "guarantee" that he will be paid if he should get injured or does not perform and thus is "cut."

Notice that a player signs not on the basis of (past) performance but on the basis he is "expected" to perform to the standards of that guaranteed contract. This is similar in professional basketball, baseball, and hockey. However, it is not the same in professional golf or tennis where you get paid after you play, based on your performance at that event. Of course, professional golfers and tennis players are individual players and do not play on a team. Therefore, a different "chemistry" is in place.

When Edwards signed with the Philadelphia Eagles as a walk-on, he signed for three years—the amount of that contract is not important because salaries in 1977 don't compare with salaries of today. He played nine years on a contract basis. The chemistry the Eagles built under the command of Head Coach Dick Vermeil created a Super Bowl contender.

Great teams that are legendary were built with "chemistry." Some of those are the Green Bay Packers of the '60s, the Dallas Cowboys of the '60s and '70s, the Minnesota Vikings, Oakland Raiders, Pittsburgh Steelers, Miami Dolphins of the '70s, and the San Francisco 49ers of the '80s. There may be others, but those legendary teams had "chemistry."

The same players stayed together year in and year out. The fans identified with them. Loyalty between fans and players becomes contagious. The players were part of the community—as a group—as a team. When Edwards played with the Eagles, the fans knew that quarterback Ron Jaworski would be throwing touchdown passes to wide receiver Harold Carmichael. That consistency becomes lost in today's game as players jump from team to team, and as a result, diminishes fan loyalty. An NFL coach needs to start over every year to re-create its team "chemistry," its culture, and fan loyalty.

People say, "Well you can't blame a player for wanting to go where he will get more money." Yes, you can! Players (not their agents) need to be held accountable for a decision to go to a team simply because of the money. Having said that, it must be emphasized that if a player feels he will have greater success and if he feels that he will be happier with another team, then a coach will say, "Go and be happy."

"Show me the money" was the catch phrase in the movie Jerry McGuire. The expression turned a lot of heads. Unfortunately, it turned the heads of young people who grew up to look at money/salaries as the benchmark for success and happiness. It can rightly be said that money can buy a lot of things, but it doesn't necessarily buy or guarantee success or happiness. Free agency may be a benefit to an individual player, but it upsets team chemistry.

Free agency has created another problem—the salary cap. The owners in the NFL are under pressure to win and win every year, and they attempt to recruit the best players available. Money, therefore, becomes key. It's a parody on the "Golden Rule," i.e., "He who has the gold, [read: most money] rules [read: can "buy" the best players available].

The salary cap causes "chemistry" problems. When a player has achieved pretty much all he is capable due to age or other factors, it is difficult to keep him on the team because of his salary needs. So often that experienced player, who can provide leadership and cohesiveness to a team, must be "cut loose." An example in 2003 was that of Emmett Smith, fourteen years with the Dallas Cowboys, being "cut loose." Later he signed a contract with the Arizona Cardinals who had "cap room," but his departure from the Cowboys was disappointing to Cowboy fans. NFL history is replete with examples of star players having to leave the team with whom they and the team had great success. Yet because of "the cap" restrictions, they had to move to another team.

Joe Montana, Ronnie Lott, and Jerry Rice wanted to remain as San Francisco 49ers; the fans loved them. Salary cap and related decisions forced management to release them. Each continued to play in the NFL (Montana with the Chiefs, Lott with the Jets and the Raiders, Rice with the Raiders). The 49er fans would have much preferred those three to stay in San Francisco; incidentally, they all continue to live in the Bay Area.

You get the point. There are many examples since 1993; almost every NFL team has lost "chemistry" because of free agency. One that affected the Jets in 2003 was the loss of Laveranues Coles, a wide receiver. Coles, in his third year with the Jets, had his best season in 2002. He caught eighty-four passes for 1,264 yards with five touchdowns. He was the Jets primary go-to guy. Every opponent in 2002 feared that Coles would "break the game open." His value during the year 2002 certainly went up. His contract for 2003 (and beyond) needed to be restructured, and general manager Terry Bradway was going to do that.

However, Coles became a free agent as of March 1, 2003, and although talks were progressing, the Washington Redskins made him an offer of $35 million for seven years, which included a $13 million signing bonus. According to NFL free agency policies, the Jets had a chance to match that offer. However, their salary-cap structure in 2001 and 2002, Edwards's first two years, was in such a way that that kind of money was not available. Plus, the Jets' present ownership and administration had inherited some salary promises committed before they took over.

So Coles had a decision to make: take the Redskins offer of $35 million or take what the Jets could afford to offer. He took the Redskins offer. Edwards holds absolutely no bad feelings for that decision. Question: Was the chemistry that Coles had developed with Pennington, the Jets starting quarterback in 2002, and the rest of the Jets receivers, Chrebet, Moss, Becht, recreated with the Redskins? Apparently, the chemistry didn't work, the Redskins didn't make the playoffs with a record five wins and eleven losses. Losing Coles and four other starters, the Jets needed to start over and create a new chemistry with new players for the 2003 season.

Free agency is a complicated issue and an intricate procedure to administer. It has created the position of "capologist" with some teams. The capologist is responsible to ensure that the team stays within the salary cap ($83 million in 2003). If a team should exceed that amount, the team must restructure its players' contract to be "under the cap" or they will incur a substantial penalty from the NFL commissioner's office. A whole group of people works in the NFL office to ensure (read: "check up on") that teams are within the salary-cap rules.

All this to operate an NFL team. Free agency and salary cap have little to do with blocking, tackling, scoring touchdowns, and winning football games. However, free agency has made "chemistry" more difficult than it ever has been in the history of the National Football

League. What Edwards endeavors to do, as a head coach (and every other head coach does similarly), is to develop a strong sense of teamwork. You do that in your family as well, as does every CEO in his or her organization. Chemistry is vital to teamwork.

And now about sportsmanship. Let's look at the importance of sportsmanship as a key element of a great team.

Paraphrasing a famous poet, "Sportsmanship—the reason there is so much sportsmanship available, is that no one ever uses it." Why is that? When Edwards accomplished something, like the "miracle" in the Meadowlands, he certainly wanted people to congratulate him. So it has been a practice of his to congratulate an opponent on a job well done. When that happens, of course, he's on the losing end. We all want to win every time. But that's unrealistic.

When we lose, can we maintain enough self-esteem to be a good sport about it—or do we let our ego get in the way? Do we think, "He was lucky to win?" Or "He got the 'breaks' or he cheated?" Is that what gets into our heads? We should celebrate our victories, but not at the expense of disrespecting our opponent. And when did all this destruction of property start? What gives anyone the right to set fire to public trash cans, overturn police cars, and throw objects at buildings or at others in the name of "celebration"?

Too often there is a lack of sportsmanship on the part of our NFL players, and Edwards constantly reminds the Jets players of their responsibility in that regard. "Trash talking," "taunting," and the like are not only degrading to your opponent, but it also puts you in a bad light. It sends the message to others that you must "profess" the act you just accomplished. To see a player make a tackle or a "sack" of the quarterback and then prance around like he just discovered a cure for cancer is not in keeping with a code of conduct to which Edwards subscribes.

The NFL Rule Book describes "unsportsmanlike conduct" (Rule 12, Section 3, Article 1, page 85) as "any act which is contrary to the generally understood principles of sportsmanship. Such acts specifically include, among others,

   a. throwing a punch or a forearm, or kicking at an opponent even though no contact is made;
   b. the use of abusive, threatening, or insulting language or gestures to opponents, teammates, game officials, or representatives of the league;

c. the use of baiting or taunting acts or words that engender ill will between teams;

d. unnecessary physical contact with a game official; and

e. removal by a player of his helmet after a play except in the bench area or during a time out.

Game officials have been instructed by the NFL commissioner and its officiating department to give close attention to the application of this rule.

Why? Why do we have to make "rules" that should be understood by each of us as common sense? While it may sound trite, "do unto others as you would like them to do unto you" is still a viable mantra. It may be trite, but it's trite because it's true. When Herman was on the playing field (circa 1977- 1987), he doesn't recall a problem among players about "taunting." Oh sure, a guy may swear at an opponent, but it usually stopped right there. With players, there was an unwritten "rule of conduct" that if a guy got out of line, as in if the guy is a "dirty" player, well, others would, sort of "take care of him."

Football is a very physical game. Unwanted acts can be "dealt with" through legal physical contact, e.g., blocking, tackling. Guys get the message quickly.

When Edwards was a player, players would not condone this current practice of standing over another player after a tackle or block, or spinning the football in his face or other acts of brashness. It just didn't happen or if it did, it was a rare occasion and was "attended to" quickly. NFL coaches have a responsibility to not only follow the rules but to also set an example of good sportsmanship. Edwards continues to do this at the Jets. His players respect his approach and philosophy of good sportsmanship.

Further, and maybe more importantly, players and coaches in the public eye are looked up to by young people. They do watch. NFL players are role models and as such carry that responsibility. Herm tells the players, "If you don't want to be a role model, then don't play in a high-class professional league, like the NFL—and by the way, don't take the big bucks they pay you." This holds true for the NBA, NHL and—yes—even college athletics. The "kids" are watching! Herm stresses this every year at his TYF (The Youth Foundation) Football Camp held in Seaside, California. If he can get the word across to eight-hundred-plus kids—and their parents, each year, maybe—just maybe—a dent in these unsportsmanlike acts that seem to get kids attention can be made.

Incidentally, TYF camp is winning that battle with the kids. They do dress differently than Herm did when he was their age, but he's impressed with their values, integrity, and sportsmanship. As an example, at the football camp kids are given shirts, shorts, and travel bags. They put their names on each of their bags, but they leave their bags and other personal items lying around as they work out at the camp. Wow! These kids come from a wide variety of backgrounds, yet they respect the rights of others. In twelve years the TYF camp has never had one—not one—personal item stolen. They are making a difference!

Respect the rights of others—that's what sportsmanship is all about. The NFL players are just "bigger kids," and that's meant with no disrespect. But they are subject to the same human frailties that younger ones are—only, at the professional level, more is expected. As example, in enforcing the "no fighting" rule, players need to be held to a consistent standard. Since "fighting" is not allowed on the field (during an NFL game), Coach Edwards does not allow it at practice. If a fight breaks out during practice, he immediately removes those two "combatants" from the field. One of two procedures is followed. The Jets have a "bubble" practice facility adjacent to their football field. Edwards has two sets of boxing gloves and dismisses those two players to that facility where they can put on the gloves and "have it out." Occasionally, however, he just sends them "to the showers." Practice is over for them on that day. In a game they will be ejected for fighting. They need to learn in practice what these consequences are.

Removing one's helmet while on the field, whether in anger or in celebration, is costly. All of the Jets coaches remind their players of that rule. While taking off one's helmet is an innocuous act in itself, the rule had to be put in because of players throwing their helmet to the ground in anger—an unsportsmanlike act.

And then it happened! First week of the season, September 8, 2002, Kansas City and Cleveland were playing. It was the last play of the game. Cleveland 39, Kansas City 37. It was Kansas City's ball second down and ten on their forty-seven yard line. The quarterback, Trent Green, dropped back to pass. Dwayne Rudd, No. 57, defensive tackle of the Browns, had the quarterback in his grasp, but Green escaped and lateraled the ball—in desperation—to Chief's tackle, John Tait, No. 76. Tait ran to the Browns, 25—a twenty-eight-yard gain. First down, except time expired on the play. Game over. But wait! Rudd, thinking that quarterback Green was sacked and didn't see Tait running with the ball, took off his helmet and threw it to the ground, presumably in celebration, while Tait was still running with the ball. The play was not over. Referee Ron Blum had no choice but to throw a flag for U-S-C (unsportsmanlike conduct). Cleveland was penalized fifteen yards. Time had expired, but the game cannot end on a foul by the defense. So the Chiefs got another play. It's called an "untimed down." Marking off half the distance from the Browns' 25 to their 12 ½, Morten Andersen kicked the field goal—"Good!" Kansas City won 40-39. Wow! Did Edwards jump on that with the players at the Jets next team meeting? They had beaten Buffalo on that Sunday in overtime and were in a celebratory mood; it was a perfect time to drive home an important lesson on the costliness of unsportsmanlike conduct.

Players want to be great; they want to play on great teams. Too often a player confuses being "famous" with being great. Herman tells his players as he tells the camp kids, being famous can happen without greatness. A guy who robs a liquor store, or beats his wife and kids, can get on television ("News at 11") or in the newspapers. Thus he can be "famous" or infamous.

To be great takes effort, commitment, preparation, self-sacrifice and determination. It's a long hard road to achieve greatness. Greatness and fame can go together, but greatness must precede any true fame.

The Official's Call

Teamwork! How often do you hear that word today? Every speech Coach Edwards and I give has an emphasis on teamwork. We don't have free agency in NFL officiating simply because there is no similar place (league) to go. However, as a referee (crew chief of seven game officials), it was my job to develop chemistry so that as a team we could go on the field with a sense of confidence in each other. Since NFL officials retire or are terminated (several every year), crews get a "rookie" (first-year official) every year. While I always welcomed a rookie into our crew, it takes on a different approach in teaching that official to work in unison with his partners.

Therefore chemistry is important to ensure excellent communication. As witnessed in recent NFL seasons, there has been a loss of communication in some NFL officiating crews. Much of this loss of communication has to do with chemistry. Since 1967, the NFL has kept its officiating crews intact throughout the season. But not in the postseason (playoff) games.

Since I started officiating in the NFL (1960), the supervisor of officials (now called the vice president of officiating) and his staff selected the playoff crews based on each individual performance by position. Hence the highest-rated referee (it's the same for other positions) is selected to officiate the Super Bowl, then on down through the other playoff games. More than likely you will have the best in their positions working as a crew in any given playoff game. Not the best (highest rated) crew. Chemistry can break down.

Starting with the 2003 season (playoffs mostly in 2004), the NFL changed the system by rewarding (assigned) its best crew to each of the playoff games. The exception is that first—and second-year officials will not be included in a playoff game crew. The league would then assign a veteran official who performed well to fill that position. This assignment by crew is an attempt to ensure communication for the playoffs. The chemistry that a crew develops during the season should serve to provide stronger communication in the postseason.

It may seem axiomatic that NFL game officials should be concerned about player conduct (i.e., sportsmanship). Unfortunately, not all officials take that extra effort to be "on top of the play"—as we call it—to maintain game control. I used the term "preventive maintenance" and each year I stressed to our crew that we all have to see "trouble" before it starts. Every official must take the responsibility of being alert to meaningless acts before they become chaos. When a fight breaks out during a game, the fans look at it as poor officiating.

Every official is encouraged to "step in" quickly to quell any disruption. Players don't really want to fight, but they have a hard time "backing down." A player doesn't want to give the appearance of being a "coward." I recall one time I stepped between two huge lineman both about 6'7" and 280-plus pounds, who had pushed—not punched—each other. I said, "Okay, okay, knock it off!" Both were steaming and ready to do combat. I continued, "That's enough!" One of the two looked (down, of course) at me and with breath that needed mouthwash, blurted out, "He pushed me first!" I laughed and thought I was back on the playground referring a little league game. Yes, as big as they may be, the "little kid" is still inside that big body.

The Prayer of a Sportsman
(author unknown)

Dear Lord, in the battle that goes on through life

I ask for a field that is fair

A chance that is equal to all in the strife

The courage to strive and to dare.

If I should win, let it be by the code

With my faith and my honor held high.

But if I should lose, let me stand by the road

And cheer as the winners go by.

CHAPTER 12

Kansas City Chiefs–2006
"I'm Baaack"

On January 9, 2006, Herman Edwards, Jr. became the Head Coach of the Kansas City Chiefs. Herm started his coaching career in 1989 with the Chiefs in the NFL's Minority Fellowship program and is the tenth head coach in the history of the Chiefs' organization.

His first job as an NFL head coach was with the New York Jets. He served in that capacity for 5 seasons, guiding the Jets to three play-off appearances, including one AFC East Division Championship. This accomplishment exceeds the record of any previous Jets' head coach.

Although much of this book is about the Jets, the real essence is the principles and philosophies of success. Herm now applies these principles and philosophies to the Chiefs' football T*E*A*M. With Coach Edwards, what you see is what you get!

The preseason analysis was that Herm, a defensive minded coach, would need to rebuild a Chiefs' defense that was lacking in the 2005 season. Herm was confident he could do that. He added veteran Ty Law who was with Herm at the Jets and brought 12 years experience along with his leadership strengths to the Chiefs' secondary.

THE 2006 PRE-SEASON

The NFL Preseason is always one of exploration. Every NFL team has 80+ professional athletes in its training camp usually beginning in mid-July and lasting until early September, when the team must establish its roster of 53 players.

Although Coach Edwards wants to look at every player on the roster to see how each plays in a real-time game, Herm also emphasizes, "You play to win the game." It is important, therefore, for the Chiefs to have some success in the preseason in order to build a winning mindset. They did, when the St. Louis Rams came to KC for the Missouri Governor's Cup and the Chiefs kept the cup with a 16-12 win. The Chiefs defeated the New Orleans Saints 10-9 two weeks later in Kansas City. (Incidentally, those same Saints played for the 2006 NFC Championship losing to the Chicago Bears who went to the Super Bowl).

Preseason scorecard: 2 wins – 2 losses.

THE CHAMPIONSHIP SEASON

That's what the NFL refers to as its league season. And that's what Coach Edwards had in mind—a championship season. Of course, All 32 head coaches had that in mind as well. So it began, Herm's first year as Chiefs' Head Coach.

GAME 1 – September 10 – Bengals at Chiefs

The Bengals were predicted by many to be the AFC representative in Super Bowl XLI. The Chiefs are 13-5 in home openers going back to 1989, but victory 'twas not to be as the Bengals won 23-10, even though the Chiefs' defense held the highly touted Bengals' offense to 236 total yards.

The major "blow" was a severe head and neck injury to starting (and all-pro) QB Trent Green. Trailing 20-3 late in the 3rd quarter, Green scrambled to pick up a first down, was late in his QB slide, and decked (but a legal tackle) by Bengals' Robert Gathers. An 11-minute delay followed as Chiefs' medical staff secured Green to a gurney to stabilize him for transportation to the hospital. Backup QB Damon Huard, who had not thrown a pass in NFL action since 2003, replaced Green.

Bengals 23, Chiefs 10 (Record: 0-1).

GAME 2 – September 17 – Chiefs at Broncos

The Broncos were favored to win the AFC West. With Huard at QB, the Chiefs went to a ground game giving the ball to RB Larry Johnson 27 times as he gained 126 yards. The Broncos made only two field goals and the Chiefs matched that for a 6-6 tie to send the game into OT. Jason Elam, who holds the NFL record for the longest field goal with Tom Dempsey at 63 yards, connected on a 39-yard game winner for a Broncos' victory.

Broncos 9, Chiefs 6 in OT (now 0-2).

GAME 3 – October 1 – 49ers at Chiefs

With a week off to heal some sore bodies, the Chiefs were ready for the San Francisco 49ers when they arrived at Arrowhead Stadium for Game 3, all but Green who was still out with the neck injury.

Damon Huard stepped up right from the start, completed his first five passes and finished the game with 18 for 23, 208 yards, two touchdowns and no interceptions. The Chiefs' defense answered the call as well by limiting the Niners to 89 yards rushing, intercepting two passes and forcing two turnovers.

Chiefs 41, 49ers 0 (now 1-2).

GAME 4 – October 8 – Chiefs at Cardinals

The Chiefs have played the Cardinals in Busch Stadium, TWA Dome, Sun Devil Stadium and now in their opening year at University of Phoenix Stadium in Glendale, Arizona. Matt Leinert, Rookie QB Heisman trophy winner from U.S.C., replaced Cardinals' veteran QB Kurt Warner throwing for two touchdowns in the first 12 minutes of the first quarter.

The Chiefs' defense stepped up to have four sacks, a blocked punt and a Ty Law interception to keep their offense on the field. With the Chiefs' offense on the field, a strong effort from RB Johnson (142 yards rushing and pass receiving), a 26 of 38 for 288 yards passing game for Huard including two TD's and zero interceptions, plus three Lawrence Tynes field goals made it possible for the Chiefs to leave Arizona with a victory.

Chiefs 23, Cardinals 20 (now 2-2).

Game 5 – October 15 – Chiefs at Steelers

Herm and the Chiefs never saw the avalanche coming. The Steelers came out blazing hot at Heintz Field. The Steelers "lit up" the scoreboard like it was a Super Bowl!

As Herm paced the sidelines he mused, "Who is that team out there playing the Steelers?" It surely wasn't the same team that he saw the last two weeks. At halftime, with the Steelers up 31-0, Coach reminded his team that, "This is not Little League when one team gets so far behind that you call the game, you have to keep playing." And they did, but the Chiefs couldn't slow down the Super Bowl Champs' offense who ran up 457 yards.

Steelers 45, Chiefs 7 (now 2-3).

"It was just one game" Coach told his team in a post game speech.

"You learn a little bit about your team in a loss like this. Don't let your mindset change, you will be better after a loss like this. You can lose your momentum, but never lose your confidence."

Game 6 – October 22 – Chargers at Chiefs

San Diego, now at six and one and leading the AFC West, came to town with its Head Coach Marty Schottenheimer. Marty was Head Coach of the Chiefs (1989 to 1998) and hired Herm as a position coach. Herm and Marty to this day remain good friends.

As they closed Friday's practice session, Herm went through a couple of housekeeping chores, e.g., Saturday's meeting times and Sunday's time schedule, then he let 'em have it—bam! "We must bring our best effort on Sunday—everyone! If you don't come to play with every ounce of your talent, you'll be standing next to me on the sidelines—no exceptions."

Sunday morning the Chiefs' locker room had a solemn quietness to it. At 11:52am—ten minutes before the coin toss—Coach entered the locker room. All players, coaches, Carl Peterson (Chiefs' President) along with Herm "took a knee." No command, no direc-tion—just a knee as a minister stood among them and asked "our God" to bless each player and their families. No pleading for "a win", just "bless us our God because we honor you." They all stood and Coach said, "Listen up—this game today will not be won in the first quarter. It just won't. You've got to play all four quarters. Don't lose your focus."

What Coach was cautioning his team was that the Chargers have a powerful offense (ranked #1 in the NFL at this point) and could easily get out ahead of the Chiefs in the score, so don't get discouraged and think the game is lost. He didn't say that! What he said was, "Don't lose your focus" or as he said in earlier chapters, "Don't give up—there's no quit in my dictionary." Simple, but powerful instructions. When the leader and the team are on the same page, short simple instructions get the job done.

The Chargers returned the opening kickoff, but LaDainian Tomilson, the Chargers' All-Pro running back, fumbled the football. "F-U-M-B-L-E!" Chiefs' ball, but all the Chiefs could settle for was a field goal attempt from 42 yards out. Tynes misses—wide left. But the Chiefs' remember Coach's words, "Don't lose your focus", and responded with three TD's—2 passing by Huard and one running, by the power of the Chiefs' running game—#27.

Halftime score—Chiefs 20, Chargers 3, as the Chiefs took advantage of San Diego's turnovers.

In the second half, Chargers come charging (sorry about that) back and eventually tied the score at 27 with 2:26 left to go in the fourth quarter. Chiefs' QB Huard went to work. With 11 seconds left and the score still 27-all, the Chiefs moved to the Chargers' 25-yard line. Third down, Tynes into kick what would be the winning field goal from the 38—a 48-yard field goal (remember, he missed a 42 yarder earlier). At the snap, the umpire blew his whistle and threw his flag. Tynes kicked it anyway —"good", but wait—no play—false start by the Chiefs' #84, which moved the ball back 5 yards. Tynes then attempted a 53-yard field goal—it's high enough and long enough—good!

"The difference was our will. It was our will today that won that game," said Coach in his post-game press conference.

Thanks Coach, that's what we say, *It's the Will, Not the Skill*. The Chargers skill was every bit as good as the Chiefs, but the victory went to the home team, whose *will* was greater.

Chiefs 30, Chargers 27 (now 3-3).

Game 7 – October 27 – Seahawks at Chiefs

Here came another Super Bowl team—the Seattle Seahawks. The 'Hawks lost to the Steelers in Super Bowl XL and were every bit as good as the Steelers that day, except on the scoreboard. The Seahawks came to Arrowhead Stadium missing two key players: QB Matt Hasselbeck and RB Shawn Alexander through injuries. The Chiefs on the other hand were healthy, except for QB Green. With Johnson rushing (155 yards) and pass catching by Tony Gonzales (116) and Eddie Kennison (132), the victory went to the Chiefs whose defense complimented that by allowing the 'Hawks only 50 rushing yards. Johnson established the Chiefs' single game record of 39 rushing attempts and was named AFC Offensive Player of the week for this performance.

You can establish yourself as a pretty good team as you approach the season's half way point and you are 4-3. "November is moving month," says Herm, "If you win in November, you usually are practicing in January." That's the Chiefs' mindset—to be practicing in January.

Chiefs 35, Seahawks 28 (now 4-3).

Game 8 – November 5 – Chiefs at St. Louis Rams

Coach Edwards is often heard shouting from the sidelines "Make a play. Make a play." And that's exactly what his team did in the first half against the Rams in Edward James Dome, resulting in a 24-10 halftime lead.

When Johnson rushes for over 100 yards (27 carries for 172 yards this day), the Chiefs are hard to beat as they won Missouri's Governor's Cup again—by defeating the Rams. (Note: It was owner Lamar Hunt's belief that each time the Kansas City [Mo.] Chiefs met a team from St. Louis [Mo.]—first the Cardinals and now the Rams—that the winner won the Governor's Cup.) One cup, but two victories in 2006.

Chiefs 31, Rams 17 (now 5-3).

Game 9 – November 12 – Chiefs at Dolphins

Coach Edwards, as Head Coach of the Jets playing in the AFC East for five seasons, knew that playing the Dolphins in Miami is "scary". Dolphins' defense had given up only 12 points in the first quarter this season. They also had beaten the Chicago Bears, who played in Super Bowl XLI. The Dolphins also had four hard running backs and good receivers.

The Chiefs didn't score until six minutes were left in the FOURTH quarter. The Dolphins' defense shut Johnson (only 75 yards) and the Chiefs' offense (265 yards) down. The Chiefs' seven penalties—very uncharacteristic of an Edwards' team—didn't help much either.

Dolphins 13, Chiefs 10 (now 5-4).

Game 10 – November 19 – Raiders at Chiefs

At 5 and 4 the Chiefs were in control of their own fate. They are now tied for the last playoff spot and needed to win. Trent Green, the Chiefs' All-Pro QB out with a severe injury since the first game, was now healthy and cleared to start the Raiders' game. The question Edwards faced all week was: do you stay with QB Huard who has guided the team to five wins or do you give Green his starting job back? Never a doubt in Edwards' mind, "Green is our starter," he said. Unfortunately, TE Gonzales, who last week moved into third place in Chiefs' history for combined net yards (8412), was hurt and did not play.

Johnson rushed for 154 yards against the Raiders' defense including two TDs, to give him 42 career rushing scores and 3rd place in Chiefs' history, as Green guided his team to victory. Although the Raiders challenged in the last minute, Chiefs' rookie safety Jarrad Page intercepted QB Aaron Brooks' pass in the end zone with 32 seconds left to seal the victory.

Chiefs 17, Raiders 13 (now 6-4).

Game 11 – November 23 – Broncos at Chiefs

You will note that this date was not a Sunday or even a Monday night game, but November 23, 2006 was historic. This was the first time in NFL history that three NFL games were played on a Thanksgiving Day. It was also historic in that the new (2006) NFL network was televising the event. The down side is that the Chiefs' owner Lamar Hunt, who campaigned to have Thanksgiving Day games (usually played in Detroit and Dallas) moved to other cities, was not in attendance. Lamar was hospitalized in Texas with prostrate cancer complications. Was he missed at this game? You bet! Was his absence and illness a motivating factor to the Chiefs? You gotta believe it was!

Arrowhead was packed—and loud, with 79,484 (largest crowd ever). The Chiefs' defense was "packed" as well, allowing the Broncos only 24 rushing yards in the first two quarters. Half time 10-3 Chiefs. "These games are never over at halftime," Coach told his team in the locker room. The Chiefs responded to Herm's encouraging words as they ran up 382 yards for a victory. Owner Lamar smiled brightly from his hospital bed.

Chiefs 19, Broncos 10 (now 7-4).

Game 12 – December 3 – Chiefs at Browns

Football is a strange game. You'd expect that with QB Green throwing for 297 yards, including four TDs, and RB Johnson gaining 110 yards and TE Gonzales catching nine passes for 105 yards, along with WR Kennison catching 7 for 117 yards that the final outcome would favor the Chiefs. However, with the Chiefs up by 14, they let the Browns off-the-hook, as backup Browns QB Derek Anderson (who?) tossed two TDs and sent the game into OT.

NFL stats show that the team who wins the coin toss usually (60%+) scores first and wins in overtime. The Chiefs won the toss, but had to punt. Browns' backup QB Anderson, subbing for injured starting QB Charlie Frye, engineered a 63-yard drive in OT for the Browns to score on a 33 yard field goal to win. "Disheartening to hold a 14-point lead and not come away with the win," Coach lamented.

Browns 31, Chiefs 28 in OT (now 7-5).

Game 13 – December 10 – Ravens at Chiefs

The disheartening loss to the Browns hung over the Chiefs' squad until about Wednesday, but Coach Edwards has a way of "moving on" and changing the team's mindset from one of despair to one of hope.

"Turnovers—fumbles and interceptions—will be key to victory against the Ravens," said Herm. And they were, but for the Ravens, not the Chiefs, as three Chiefs' first half turnovers stopped their offense cold. The "Hot" Chiefs' consecutive home wins (18) in the month of December turned as cold as the weather does in K.C. that time of year.

Ravens 20, Chiefs 10 (now 7-6).

Game 14 – December 17 – Chiefs at Chargers

It looked to be an exciting game-of-the-week type atmosphere in San Diego. An NFL Sunday Night Game (Al Michaels and John Madden on NBC), the Chargers' record was 11 and 2, having won seven straight. "This is a playoff game for us," Coach Edwards told his team.

The shocker, however, came on Wednesday of that week, when the founder of the Chiefs, Lamar Hunt, succumbed to the cancer he had been battling. And "battling" is the most apt word that comes to mind when talking about Hunt. Born to Texas oil-magnate, H.L. Hunt, Lamar never basked in the luxury of his billionaire father. As an example, when Lamar flew on a commercial airline, he flew "coach"!

There are many outstanding owners who made professional football what it is today—Lamar Hunt might well stand at the head of that class. Lamar's death hit the entire Chiefs' family HARD. Everyone from groundskeepers to President Carl Peterson was hurting with this loss. Lamar was not only a visible owner, but touched everyone with his humanness and humility; he was a lamplighter who left a legacy that will be difficult to match.

Was the Chargers' game, then, to be an incentive for victory for the Chiefs? You bet! The Chargers, having loss to the Chiefs in October and now with a nationwide television audience watching, indeed, had an (almost) equal incentive. RB Johnson was held to 84 yards rushing and QB Green was 23-41 for 185 yards, no TDs and one interception. With San Diego's RB Tomlinson rushing for almost 200 yards (199), the Chargers controlled the game to win. The Chiefs have now lost three straight—and their owner!

Chargers 20, Chiefs 9 (now 7-7).

Game 15 – December 27 – Chiefs at Raiders

The Chiefs were now on the "bubble" and had to win to make the playoffs as a wildcard.

Coach Edwards NEVER gets "down" on his team, yet he said publicly "We're struggling right now—we can't score" (having only scored 19 points in the last two games and having lost three in a row). The players, if they didn't hear him say that, at least felt it and "stepped up" to have a good week of practice.

The Chiefs' offense scored 20 points in McAfee Coliseum (more than the two previous games combined). Johnson had 31 carries for 135 yards, which gave him a season high of 371 to break former All-Pro Chiefs' RB Christian Okoye's record. Safety Jarrad Page intercepted Raiders' QB Andrew Walter twice, the last one ending a fourth quarter Raiders' surge.

Chiefs 20, Raiders 9 (now 8-7).

Game 16 – December 31 – Jaguars at Chiefs

The playoff picture was very "IFFY" on this last day of the year. If the Chiefs win and three other teams (Jaguars, Ravens and Bengals), who had a "shot" at the second wildcard spot lose, the Chiefs would be the #8 seed in the playoffs.

The Jags are a tough, physical team, but Herm is still shouting from the sidelines, "Make-a-play, make-a-play." And Rookie Bernard Pollard did just that! Early in the first quarter he blocked Chris Hanson's punt and fell on it in the end zone. Chiefs 7, Jacksonville 0—Good start!

Although the Jags trimmed the Chiefs' lead to 35-30, the Chiefs got the ball and turned to Mr. Reliable, Larry Johnson, who ate up the clock for a Chiefs' victory—and a PLAYOFF BERTH. The other three teams, who could have had that final playoff spot, all lost. Coach Edwards now fits in a special class—one of two NFL coaches to lead two teams to the playoffs in their first season as Head Coach.

Chiefs 35, Jags 30 (now 9-7).

AFC WILD CARD PLAYOFF January 6 – Chiefs at Colts

As you read in Chapter 10, Coach Edwards says, "You want to be practicing in January." And the Chiefs were as the #8 seed in the eight team AFC playoffs. Of course, being #8 they had to play #1 in #1's house. And there they were—the 12 and 4 Indianapolis Colts. Almost as important, Herm would again face his close friend and mentor, Tony Dungy, the Colts' Head Coach. If there was ever a healthier competition and sportsmanlike relationship in the NFL, I have not seen it. These two coaches love to win—hate to lose, but would never think of doing anything unethical to win. And, when it's all over, are the best of friends. That's the way they operate their lives and teach competitive professional football to their athletes.

The Chiefs' offense never got in sync in the RCA Dome as they went "3 and out" on each of their six first half possessions and the Colts took advantage with kicker Adam Vinateri connecting on three fields goals for a 9-0 lead at halftime. When RB Johnson goes 13 for 32 yards, TE Gonzales only four catches for 25 yards, and a blank—zero catches—for WR Kennison, it was easy to figure that the Colts' defense, which had been suspect all season, came to play.

The Chiefs' defense did its part as they held the Colts'—the NFL's 3rd ranked offense—out of the end zone for over 40 minutes and—get this—intercepted QB Peyton Manning three times! (The Colts, as you know, advanced to Super Bowl XLI and beat the NFC Chicago Bears at Dolphins Stadium with Manning as MVP!)

"Getting to the playoffs is what makes this (NFL) game fun," said Coach Edwards. 'Course if you were to ask him, he would certainly say, winning playoff games is even "funner" (my word, not his). Herm concludes, "The playoffs are refreshing. Players need to 'taste' it. It's a great stepping stone."

Coach, we will enjoy watching you guide your T*E*A*M across to the next stepping stone in 2007 and beyond.

Epilogue – The Official's Call

The unfortunate passing of Chiefs' Owner Lamar Hunt took some of the luster off a successful first season for Coach Edwards. Hunt would have shaken the hand of every Chiefs' player, every Chiefs' coach as well as every employee and that of Head Coach Herm Edwards, to congratulate them ALL for living up to the standards he established when he put the Chiefs in Kansas City.

Every NFL official who has ever worked a Chiefs' game either at Arrowhead or on the road had the highest respect for Lamar Hunt. Yet, there is not and never will be—a favorable (prejudiced) "call" go in Chiefs' favor because of Mr. Hunt or the positivity of Coach Herm Edwards. Officials know that with Coach Edwards on the sidelines he expects of them the same as he does of his players, his coaches and himself, to wit:

Be on time

Be prepared

Don't quit

Respect the game—and every player

Leave the game better than you found it.

Now, I ask you to go to page 188 to read "Broomsweeps."

<u>Epilogue II</u>

Now that you have come to know Coach Edwards and learn that "what you see is what you get," please notice in #5 (above) that he does, indeed, "leave the game better." The 2006 Chiefs improved over the 2005 season in defense in three areas of NFL team rankings:

Total yards allowed per game from 25th to 16th

Passing yards allowed per game from 30th to 18th

Points allowed per game from 16th to 11th

Also, on his personal side Herm improved his family by the addition of Vivian born August 2006 who joins Mother (Lia) and Dad along with older sister Gabrielle.

Coach Edwards along with President Peterson, and with the advice of his coaches and scouts, drafted WR Dwayne Bowe in the first round of the 2007 NFL Draft to add some passing threat to go with the strong running game of All-Pro Larry Johnson and then drafted Rookie RB Kolby Smith to further strengthen that aspect of their game. Knowing that All-Pro Trent Green was 37, Coach decided to go with veteran Damon Huard, and Brodie Coyle, a second year QB from Alabama. Coach Edwards asks of his quarterbacks, "Just manage the game. You don't have to win it (by yourself)." He continues, "On offense, if we can commit less than three turnovers (i.e. fumbles, interceptions) per game, we have a good chance of winning."

The Chiefs traded two veteran players, Green went to the Miami

Dolphins, and WR/Punt Returner Dante Hall, to the St. Louis Rams for two-2007 Draft picks, one of which was Smith. Coach hopes that Rookie Ean Randolph, a shifty kick returner with blazing speed and who earned Big East Special Teams Player of the Year from South Florida, will pick up their punt return game. Kicker Laurence Tynes requested to move on as well and went to the NY Giants, so the Chiefs drafted kicker Justin Medlock, who had a successful career at UCLA. Two defensive lineman, DE Claude Martin and DR Demarcus Tyler, were drafted to help an improving defense.

Broom Sweeps

These are pertinent sayings—I call them "Broom Sweeps" (because of the "broom") that are created to serve as reminders about the intention of goodness in sports.

- What'll I do on Sunday? (Regarding the NFL decision not to have games on Sunday following the 9/11 terrorist attack) Tell 'em to go to church.
- Excellence is good; exemplary is better.
- You gotta get the corners.
- Don't be afraid of the broom.
- Get out son; we gotta look to the east.
- There's a reason for everything.
- You can call me Mr. Bob.
- He shouldn't have played that long. He wasn't that good. They just could never get rid of him. He was such a fierce competitor.
- Don't give up.
- It just shows what perseverance gets you when you believe in each other.
- Quit. There's no "quit" in my dictionary.
- The only time you quit is when you retire.
- When you lose focus on what you're doing, it's no good.
- Don't panic. Whatever you do, don't panic.
- When you start pointing fingers, there will be three pointing back at you.
- You can lose your momentum, but never lose your confidence.

- Coach, you can't do that [walk out on your players], you got to enjoy the game (Herman was eighteen years old when he said this to his coach).
- You've got to cut some people. That's the toughest thing for a coach.
- The possibilities always lie ahead of you, not behind you.
- Let's look for the next one. There's something good up ahead.
- The effort is what it is.
- My attitude is "just show me an opportunity. I'll work for it."
- The guys had their heads down at halftime. I told them, "Keep your heads up. We're gonna win this game," and we did.
- I'm glad we won, but I'm also proud that we're not satisfied.
- Never let 'em see you sweat.
- Never let anybody steal your grin.
- Quit. Not on my watch.
- Be on time.
- They'd be runnin' hundreds—over and over. At first I thought that's all they're doing. I soon learned they were just coolin' down.
- Dance in the end zone? This is a game of respect, and we shouldn't belittle each other.
- You're special. You've got a gift.
- Did I leave this game better?
- Nothin' good happens after midnight.
- Being on time is a unifying factor.
- Be on time. No excuses. No exceptions.
- You must think of yourself as a winner now!
- Always do the right thing.
- Get clear. Get confident.
- Communication is not a passive exercise.
- We—not I.
- Talk with your players (kids/employees) not at them.
- Mental toughness = self-control plus focus.
- Play fast, play hard, play smart.
- Practice doesn't make perfect; only perfect practice makes perfect.
- T-E-A-M—Together Everyone Accomplishes More
- Every player must "buy into" every play.
- If they believe in me and my motives, then there is unity.
- Stress doesn't kill you. Distress may.

- The mind by its very nature is a goal-setting machine.
- Most of us die with our music still in us.
- He absolutely leads by example.
- You play for the logo on your helmet, not the name on the back of your jersey.
- We'd go "bang up" on everybody we knew (to get donations for our golf tournament).
- Give me a "Ben Franklin"; it was always a $100 we would ask for.
- When you are doing the right thing, good things will happen.
- I am not the sole cause.
- Chemistry, yeah, chemistry. That's it.
- I look each one in the eye—then I can trust.
- People don't care how much you know until they know how much you care.
- Nurturing is one of caring.
- Show me the money.
- We play to win the game.
- Hope! That's what it's all about.
- Here's what we gotta do.
- I think you need to learn how to handle losing before you can win.
- Keep hope alive.
- Father to son: "We don't have a lot of money, but the one thing I can give you is a good name; do the best you can with it."
- Help me help you.
- Attitude: Thoughts of the heart.
- Leadership is not so much about ability but more about responsibility.
- Character is what you do when nobody's watching
- Sportsmanship is what you do when everybody's watching
- On giving back: I can't do all my community needs. But my community needs all I can do.
- Diversity is important. Without unity, however, it is of little value.
- Confidence is when you're down two scores in the fourth quarter and you still believe you will win.
- To the world you might be just one person. But to one person you might be the world.

IF

If you can keep your head when all about you are losing theirs and blaming it on you,

If you can trust yourself when all men doubt you, but make allowance for their doubting, too:

If you can wait and not be tired by waiting, or, being lied about, don't deal in lies; or, being hated, don't give way to hating, and yet don't look too good, not talk too wise.

If you can dream–and not make dreams your master; if you can think–and not make thought your aim,
If you can meet with triumph and disaster and treat those two imposters just the same;

If you can bear to hear the truth you've spoken twisted by knaves to make a trap for fools, or watch the things you gave your life to broken, and stoop and build them up with worn out tools,

If you can make one heap of all your winnings and risk it all on one turn of pitch-and-toss, and lose, and start again at your beginnings, and never breathe a word about your loss,

If you can force your heart and nerve and sinew to serve your turn long after they are gone, and so hold on when there is nothing in you except the will which says to them–"hold on!"

If you can talk with crowds and keep your virtue, or walk with kings–nor lose the common touch.

If neither foes nor loving friends can hurt you, if all men count with you but none too much;

If you can fill the unforgiving minute with sixty seconds' worth of distance run,

Yours is the Earth and everything that's in it, and, which is more–you'll be a man, my son.

–**Rudyard Kipling**

ABOUT JIM TUNNEY

Jim Tunney has had an exemplary career in sports. A former high school coach, teacher, principal and district superintendent, he had a forty-year career in officiating football and basketball. Thirty-one of those years he was an NFL referee working a record twenty-nine postseason games including three Super Bowls, ten NFC/AFC championship games, six Pro Bowls, and twenty-five Monday-night games. He officiated some of the most memorable games in NFL history, including "The Ice Bowl," "The Kick," "The 100th Bears-Packers Game," "The Snowball Game," the "Final Fumble," "The Fog Bowl," and "The Catch." His book *Impartial Judgment: The "Dean of NFL Referees" Calls Pro Football as He Sees It*, chronicles his NFL career.

As a professional speaker, he is past president of the National Speakers Association and a charter member of its most prestigious group, the CPAE Speakers Hall of Fame. Jim holds every professional designation of the NSA, including the "Oscar" of Professional Speaking—the Cavett.

Dr. Tunney, a doctorate in education from University of Southern California, continues to serve his community as a Trustee of Monterey Peninsula College (10 years) and a Trustee Emeritus at York School, where he once served as Headmaster. In 1993, he founded the Jim Tunney Youth Foundation to support local community programs that develop leadership, work skills, wellness, and self-esteem in youth. In 2007 NSA named him "Philanthropist of the Year." He and his wife, Linda, live in Pebble Beach, California. They have six children and sixteen grandchildren.

As an author he has written and/or co-authored eight books: *Impartial Judgment, Chicken Soup for the Sports Fan's Soul, Speaking Secrets of the Masters, You Can Do It!, Super Bowl Sunday, Insights into Excellence, Lessons in Leadership,* and *Build a Better You.*

His *On the Tunney Side of the Street* is a weekly newspaper column also available via e-mail. Look for his soon to be released book,

On the Tunney Side of the Street, featuring the best of his newspaper columns that takes examples from the world of sports to help people improve their lives.

Jim Tunney Associates
PO Box 1500
Carmel-by-the-Sea, California, 93921
www.jimtunney.com
e-mail: jim@jimtunney.com

ABOUT THE JIM TUNNEY
YOUTH FOUNDATION

Established in June, 1993, the Jim Tunney Youth Foundation supports community programs and resources that work with youth to develop leadership, work skills, wellness, and self-esteem. We emphasize programs that work one-on-one with kids, not just to identify problems that hinder, but also to illuminate possibilities and increase realistic options for building productive, self-determining lives.

We do not restrict our support to one kind of program. A grant might be made to purchase sports or computer equipment, or to support an earned-reward program that teaches goal setting, or any of a wide-range of possibilities. We look for programs that emphasizes skills and that develop the understanding that commitment and discipline benefit dreams.

Founded by former NFL referee and educator Jim Tunney, we are governed by a board of directors comprised of community leaders with deep experience in education, business and community programs. Funded by private and corporate contributions, the Jim Tunney Youth Foundation is a fully tax deductible 501(c)(3) nonprofit organization.

• LEADERSHIP • WORK SKILLS • WELLNESS
• SELF- ESTEEM

JIM TUNNEY YOUTH FOUNDATION
BOARD OF DIRECTORS:

Mason Case	Ron Johnson
Mike Chapman	Clay Larson
Herm Edwards	Herb Lister
Jim Griggs	Lawson Little
Marilynn Gustafson	Ken Schley
Shari Hastey	Gordon Paul Smith
Marcy Hyman	John Staples (Emeritus)
Bob Infelise	Linda Tunney

Proceeds from *It's the Will, Not the Skill* will be donated to the Jim Tunney Youth Foundation.